A

MOMENT IN TIME
WITH GOD

(Collection of short stories, poems,
and dreams)

By
Claudette Miller

Plus Poems written by Ron Massman

PRESS

www.xulonpress.com

Pat

May you be
blessed as you
read the words
of this book.

Claudette

DEDICATION

The following poem is a tribute to my husband, Glenn Terry Miller, who went to be with the Lord on May 31, 2001.

GOODBYE MY LOVE

We walked this path hand in hand.
Our hearts were knit together as one.
We faced the storms of life as one mighty force.
You and me, stood as one against the world.
We lifted each other up in times of weakness.
We completed each other.
What one lacked, the other had in plenty.
We celebrated our victories.
We shared our dreams.
We traveled through the valleys.
We stood on the mountaintops.
We were best of friends.
The bond of our love could not be broken.

Time came when sickness invaded your body.
We fought the good fight of faith.
You held on and would not let go.
You became tired and weak.
But still you would not give up.
I prayed to God:
"If he wants to go, I release my Love to you."
Then you were gone.
The memory of our love will never be forgotten.
Until I see you again in Heaven.
Goodbye my Love.

ACKNOWLEDGEMENTS

I am very grateful to my daughter , Kelly Roddy, and her husband, Roosevelt Roddy III for asking me to live with them and allowing me to invest in the lives of my two grandchildren, Javon and Samara Roddy. Their love and support has given me the opportunity to heal.

I have been blessed to know Tina Patterson as an incredible friend for twenty years. She has been with me through the difficult times and the good times. I remember when my husband, Glenn, was rushed to the hospital. Tina and her husband postponed their vacation plans to be with me. When my husband passed away, Tina and Larry took me on a trip to Galveston for a week where the sound of the ocean brought peace to my heart. As my agent, Tina has motivated me to continue with this book when I felt overwhelmed and wanted to give up.

I felt privileged and honored when Ron Massman agreed to share his poignant poems with me and allowed me to publish them in this book. I met Ron and his wife, Linda, after my husband passed away. My life has been enhanced by their friendship.

I want to thank Shae Hamrick, my editor, for her commitment, encouragement, and patience. There were moments when I was unable to wrap my brain around what she was trying to teach me. She kept me on the path and showed me how to cross the finish line.

I have been privileged to sit under the teachings of some anointed pastors and their wives: Pastor Gary and April (Osteen) Simons of High Point Church in Arlington, Texas; Pastor Jim and Mary-Louise Cox of Church on the Rock in Bellmead, Texas; and Pastor Ronnie and Kim Holmes of Church of the Open Door in Waco, Texas. These pastors have fed me the meat of God's word, which allowed me to stand strong during the storms of life.

I would be amiss if I neglected to acknowledge those who helped me feel like a princess for the photo on the back cover of this book: Laura Montoya from *A Salon by Joni* in Hewitt, Texas; Georgia Baird, Independent Sales Director for *Mary Kay Cosmetics*; and Karyn Turnbull with *Portrait Innovations*, Waco, Texas. We had so much fun.

Thank you,
Claudette Miller

TABLE OF CONTENTS

INTRODUCTION

Never in my wildest dreams did I ever think I would be writing a book. In 2001, I lost my husband to a serious illness. Since then, my brother has died of an unexpected massive heart attack at age 55, my second marriage ended in divorce, and my son has decided to dissolve any contact with my family. As a result of all this my own health became precarious.

For me, I knew that the only way I could stand through it all was to hold on (spiritually) with bulldog tenacity to the hem of my Lord's garment. He has brought me through so much.

In January of 2008, I told the Lord that I wanted to express my love to Him in words. The poem, "A Moment in Time," was the product of this desire. But it didn't stop there. God compelled me to write. He would wake me up in the middle of the night with words to write down. After two years of writing anything and everything, God has encouraged me to put the writings in a book.

This book is a combination of my devotional time with God and my testimony, which includes poems, prose, stories, dreams and prophecies. I know in my heart that what is written on the pages of this book is not from me, but from God. I have made my life transparent by sharing the valleys and the mountains I have walked through. As I share these words with the reader, I hope they will be a blessing.

GOOD MORNING LORD

SCRIPTURES:

Your word is a lamp to my feet and a light to my path. (Psalm 119:105)

This Book of the Law shall not depart from your mouth, but you shall meditate in it day and night, that you may observe to do according to all that is written in it. For then you will make your way prosperous, and then you will have good success. (Joshua 1:8)

This morning, the first words on my lips were, "Good morning, Lord. Thank you for another day." With a cup of coffee in one hand and my Bible in the other, I eased into the recliner. I was anxious for our special time together. I have learned that my days are not the same without first taking time for you.

Finding the place in my Bible where I had finished reading yesterday, I read your Word. Everything around me disappeared and I was drawn into the world of Bible. I could visualize the people and sense the emotions they felt. The words stood out on the page in bold black letters and I heard your tender voice in my heart. The nuggets of insight spoke volumes to me. I wrote in my journal what you showed me. When I was done, I knew I could face anything that I encountered during the day.

Your Word tells me you are a just and righteous God full of love, mercy, and compassion. Your Word tells me all that Jesus bought for me with His life. Your Word tells me who I am and how I can face each day in victory. Your Word shows me the difference between right and wrong. Your Word is alive and pertinent for today. If I am afraid, depressed, lonely, worried, lost, angry, confused, addicted, or sick, the answer is in your Word, the Bible.

FOOD FOR THOUGHT: God desires to spend time together in the Word with us. I pray that our hunger for the Word will grow. As we read your Word, I ask that you will reveal yourself to us and that your Word draws us closer to you. I pray that your Word shows us the areas we need to change so that our lives will please you.

GOD REJOICES OVER HIS CHILDREN

SCRIPTURES:

Do not fear, little flock, for it is your Father's good pleasure to give you the kingdom. (Luke 12:32)

Let the Lord be magnified, who has pleasure in the prosperity of His servant. (Psalm 35:27b)

For the Lord takes pleasure in His people. (Psalm 149:4)

I observe the whole world, searching for people who take time to acknowledge and reverence me, Jehovah God. I have abundant, overflowing blessings I am prepared to bestow on those who desire to know me and walk in my truths.

My heart beats with joy when one of my children wants to sit on my lap for a while and fellowship with me. I smile when they take time to enjoy the good things of life that I created for their pleasure, such as watching a beautiful sunset, smelling the flowers, or savoring the flavor of the scrumptious fruits and vegetables I prepared for them.

I am proud when my children ask for my help, realizing that I want to provide for them. When they are afraid or overwhelmed, I whisper in their ear, "Do not fear, I will never forsake you."

19

Just as you place your photos in an album, I have a book of remembrance for those who meditate on my name (see Malachi 3:16). I see your tears and put them in a bottle (see Psalm 56:8). I care about every aspect of your life, big or small.

Just as a parent's heart beats for his child, my heart longs for you. I love you so much that I sent my only son, Jesus, to Earth so that He could redeem you from the enemy (see John 3:16). You are more important to me than you will ever know.

When you sing praises, all of Heaven rejoices with you. When you worship from your heart, I bend over my throne to listen closer. When I hear you say "Daddy", you have my compete attention.

I anxiously wait to see you face to face, when the veil of human flesh is taken from your eyes and you see me fully.

Your loving Father, God.

FOOD FOR THOUGHT: Jehovah, sometimes we do not fully comprehend how much you love us. We have mistakenly perceived that you are ready with a rod to scold us when we make a mistake. As a loving and righteous Father, you desire to raise us to fruition, bringing pleasure and glory to you.

DADDY'S LITTLE GIRL

SCRIPTURE:

The Father loves the Son and has given all things into His hand. (John 3:35)

I was looking out my window today, and I saw a little girl walking with her daddy. Her little hand was completely engulfed in her father's hand. Oh, how he towered above her, like a strong tower of protection. The little girl was looking up at her daddy. She was so proud. And she felt so safe. She knew her daddy could handle the giants.

I turned to watch my granddaughter. She had crawled up in her daddy's lap. She held her father's face in her little hands. As she looked at her father with eyes of joy, she said, "I love you, Daddy." Oh, how precious was that moment. Her daddy was her "knight in shining armor."

As a little girl, my daddy had a special place in my heart. I had placed him on a pedestal. To me, he could do no wrong. He was a very hard worker and he had wisdom and discernment that drew many people to him. In my eyes, he knew everything. Oh, how I wanted to please him.

Sometimes I wish I was that little girl again, knowing my daddy was there to protect me from the storms of life. Then I heard the gentle voice of my heavenly Father, "I love you more than you will ever know. I will never leave you. Let me hold your hand, and I will be your strong tower of protection."

There is nothing like a father's love. Some of us may have had a good father figure, while others may have had a bad father figure. Either way, they are men with earthly temples, subject to how they handle the problems of life. However, no man on Earth can compare to our heavenly Father. He is holy, just, righteous, and trustworthy. He never changes. He is the same yesterday, today and tomorrow.

FOOD FOR THOUGHT: For those who have been wounded by their earthly fathers, I ask God to bring the healing needed so they can surrender their lives completely to their heavenly Father. For those who have known a good father, I ask the Holy Spirit to help us to remember to honor our heavenly Father. He is the "best daddy".

HE KNOWS MY NAME

SCRIPTURES:

See, I have inscribed you on the palms of My hands. (Isaiah 49:16)

But the very hairs of your head are all numbered. (Matthew 10:30)

For you formed my inward parts; You covered me in my mother's womb. (Psalm 139:13)

Do you hear your heavenly Father when He calls your name? Sometimes He softly calls your name, as in a whisper. Then there are times He may boldly say your name, as if to get your attention. But are we listening to when He calls us?

When my children were little, sometimes I would tune them out. They would be talking to me, but my brain would not digest what they were saying. Are we guilty of the same thing with God? Are our lives so busy that we don't hear God when He calls our name?

In Samuel 3:1-5 it reads: "Now the boy Samuel ministered to the Lord before Eli. And the word of the Lord was rare in those days; there was no widespread revelation. And it came to pass at that time, while Eli was lying down in his place, and when his eyes had begun to grow so dim that he could not see, and before the lamp of God went out in the tabernacle of the Lord where the ark of God was, and while Samuel was lying down, that the Lord called Samuel, and he answered, 'Here I am!' So he ran to Eli and said, 'Here I am for you called me.' And he said 'I did not call you.'"

As the narrative continues, this happened several times before Eli, the prophet, realized that God was speaking to Samuel. So Eli told Samuel the next time he heard God say, "Samuel," he should tell God, "Here I am."

Can you imagine that the creator of the universe knows our name? He even knows the number of the hairs on our heads. He knew us when we were in our mother's womb. We could respond by saying that God is omniscient; therefore, He should know our name. But I think there is something personal when someone calls me by my name. I like to hear God say my name. That means He is personally talking to me, not someone else.

When God calls my name, I want to make sure that I am available and that I can hear Him when He calls. I want to be alert and respond to Him. He may be telling me something very important that I need to know. Or He could be showing me an area in my life that needs correction. Or He may be speaking words of encouragement. When God speaks to me, I want to hear Him.

FOOD FOR THOUGHT: I pray that we are alert and attentive to the voice of God so that we can hear Him when He calls our name. I also pray that we will respond to God and say "Here I am."

SPIRITUAL HAPPY BIRTHDAY
(My Testimony)

SCRIPTURE:

Jesus answered and said to him [Nicodemus], "Most assuredly, I say to you, unless one is born again, he cannot see the kingdom of God." (John 3:3)

On June 10, 1977 at the age of 29 I became a born again Christian. Up until that very special day, I had never heard the words "born again." I was raised in the Catholic doctrine. I loved God, but I did not know God personally.

When I went to college in 1966, I entered a world I was not prepared to face. I felt lost and over-whelmed. Then the day came when an unbearable, painful event caused me to tell God, "If you can allow such a horrible thing happen to me, I don't want to know you." As an angry person, I walked away from God, embracing whatever the world brought my way. But a loving and merciful God sought me even when I was not seeking Him.

In 1977, I had been married three years. We had a one year old baby girl. My husband, Glenn, and I both worked a fulltime day job. As our nighttime job, we were invited into peoples' homes to put on dinners that were cooked with waterless cookware. Glenn did the demonstration and I did the clean up.

One night we served a dinner in a Christian home. The couples shared with each other about what Jesus had done in their lives. They did not try to evangelize us. They just talked to each other openly about Jesus. They enjoyed a peace and love I did not have. This dinner led to two more dinners. Again, the people shared with each other about the goodness of God. I witnessed a love that was calling me.

On the way home from the third dinner, I told my husband that these people had a joy I needed. Even though Glenn was not a Christian at the time, he persuaded me to return to the house. I was nervous, but the love of God these people shared with each other drew me in like a magnet. As the host opened the door, I blurted out, "I want and need what you have." They gladly shared with me the salvation story and what it meant to be born again. That night I accepted Jesus as my Lord and Savior.

I immediately knew something was different. I felt a love that was beyond measure. I wanted to know why I had not heard about this fantastic experience of being born again. I thought I had received the greatest gift and I wanted to tell the whole world.

Now every June 10th, I celebrate my birthday; not my physical birth, but my spiritual birth.

FOOD FOR THOUGHT: Abba Father, thank you for loving me and seeking me even after I walked away from you. I believe in my heart the dinners we performed in those homes were part of your plan to draw me back to you. I was like the "lost sheep" and you came after me. You love each and every person that has been born physically into this world, no matter what that person has done. You will continually seek the lost. I pray the reader will know the special love that only can be found by knowing God.

NEW BEGINNINGS

SCRIPTURE:

Therefore, if anyone is in Christ, he is a new creation, old things have passed away; behold all things have become new. (2 Corinthians 5:17)

We begin each New Year with anticipation that this year will be different. With our list of resolutions, we have new hope that we are starting the year afresh with a clean slate. In most cases, we slip or mess up and then we let the failure live with us until the next year, when we begin the same scenario all over again.

When we are born again we become a new creature in Christ. God tells us in Isaiah 43:26, "I, even I, am He who blots out your transgressions for My own sake; and *I will not remember your sins.*" The past is behind us and we wake up each new morning, knowing we start the day with a clean slate, even if we messed up the day before. We don't have to wait a whole year.

The Word of God says it best..."But when the kindness and the love of God our Savior toward man appeared, not by works of righteousness which we have done, but according to His mercy He saved us, *through the washing of regeneration and renewing of the Holy Spirit*, whom He poured out on us abundantly through Jesus Christ our Savior" (Titus 3:4-6).

"I beseech you therefore, brethren, by the mercies of God, that you present your bodies a living sacrifice, holy, acceptable to God, which is your reasonable service. And do not be conformed to this world, but be *transformed by the renewing of your mind*, that you may prove what is that good and acceptable and perfect will of God" (Romans 12:1-2).

I can testify that I am not the same person I was thirty-three years ago when I became born again. It has been a slow, gradual process. Sometimes it has been two steps forward and one step back. But I have been changed by the transforming of my mind through the Word with help of the Holy Spirit, who lives in me. "But we all, with unveiled face, beholding as in a mirror the glory of the Lord, are *being transformed into the same image from glory to glory, just as by the Spirit of the Lord*" (2 Corinthians 3:18).

FOOD FOR THOUGHT: Father, thank you for Jesus who, because of the cross, has wiped away my past and allowed me to start each new day with a clean slate. Thank you for the Holy Spirit and the Word that transforms and renews my mind from the old ways of world thinking to your way of thinking. You are the only One who can change me.

OPEN DOOR TO THE FATHER

SCRIPTURES:

Behold, I stand at the door and knock. If anyone hears My voice and opens the door, I will come in to him and dine with him, and he with Me. (Revelation 3:20)

Let us therefore come boldly to the throne of grace that we may obtain mercy and find grace to help in time of need. (Hebrews 4:16)

One night as I was lying in bed, I was immersed in my thoughts and worries. I realized I needed to go to God in prayer. I needed to knock on God's door, just like a child may knock on an earthly father's bedroom or study door to gain entrance. In a momentary vision from the Holy Spirit, I saw myself raising my hand to knock on the door; however, before I was able to knock, I heard God say, "The door is already open."

The insight of this simple phrase spoke volumes to me. When I originally accepted Jesus as my savior, I answered the call of God knocking on the door of my heart. I opened the door to Him, allowing Him to enter. God became my Father. After that I had the right to come boldly to my heavenly Father anytime; similar to a child coming to a loving, earthly Father.

God says His door is always open to His children. He wants and waits for His children to come and sit at His feet and talk with Him. These are special times when a child and a Father visit with each other. We can cry together at times of pain. (And believe me, God does cry with us when we are hurting.) We can even laugh together at funny moments in our life. We can rejoice with Him over His protection and provision. We can ask God for His wisdom and help in everyday matters. Or there are times when we can just be quiet and listen to the sound of His voice, to the sound of His heart-beat, and get to know who God is and how much He loves us.

FOOD FOR THOUGHT: As a child of God, our heavenly Father says we can boldly go to Him, anytime, without fear, but with reverence. He desires to fellowship with His children. The door is open. I pray we develop this relationship and the pathway becomes worn by our continuously going to Him.

HIS LOVE

When weary and worn with no hope for tomorrow,
There's one God who knows what will be;
It's Jesus my Lord and His prayers to my Father,
His Love: Voiced at Gethsemane.

When tossed to-and-fro in life's ocean of doubt,
There's one God on whom I can stand;
In Jesus my Lord and His prayers to my Father,
His Love: See the nails on His hands.

When a need then arises that I cannot conquer,
There's one God to whom I can pray;
Through Jesus my Lord and His prayers to my Father,
His Love: See Him carried away.

When joy floods my soul in those moments of blessing,
There's one God for whom praises flow;
To Jesus my Lord and His prayers to my Father,
His Love: Risen proof for my soul!

By Ron Massman

CROSSING OVER THE JORDAN RIVER

SCRIPTURE:

So it was, when the people set out from their camp to cross over the Jordan, with the priests bearing the ark of the covenant before the people, and as those who bore the ark came to the Jordan, and the feet of the priests who bore the ark dipped in the edge of the water (for the Jordan overflows all its banks during the whole time of harvest), that the waters which came down from upstream stood still, and rose in a heap very far away at Adam... Then the priests who bore the ark of the covenant of the Lord stood firm on dry ground in the midst of the Jordan; and all Israel crossed over on dry ground, until all the people had crossed completely over the Jordan. (Joshua 3:14-17)

In order to reach the Promise Land in our lives, we sometimes have a Jordan River to cross. There may be obstacles in our paths that block us from going forward – a *physical* obstacle, such as lack of money, or a *spiritual* obstacle, such as fear of the unknown. But God wants us to possess the land, to possess the promises He has given us in His Word.

In spiritual terms, you may be standing on one side of the river that is separating you from the Promise Land you want to possess. You wonder how you are going to cross the river. First, before you go forward, you need a word from God. What does God say you need to do in order to possess the land? For example, if you need healing, are you doing what is needed to walk in divine health? There are both *spiritual* and *physical* things you need to do: 1) speak the Word of God regarding healing, and 2) eat right, exercise, reduce the stress, and rest. Another example is if you want to become debt free, again there are *spiritual* and *physical* things you need to do: 1) give tithes and offerings, and 2) monitor your spending and not use credit cards frivolously.

The next step involves going forward in faith by obediently doing what God tells you to do. Just like the Israelites did when crossing the Jordan River, God told them that as soon as the feet of the priests who bore the ark touched the water, the waters which came down from upstream would stand still. The river was not going to stop flowing until the soles of the feet of the priests touched the waters. So by faith that is exactly what the priests did. When they took the step forward, the waters parted and the people crossed over on dry ground. Please note that the Bible says the waters rose in a heap very far away at a city named Adam on the other side of the river. The waters didn't pile up in a heap in front of them, but far away at Adam. I wonder how long it took from when the priests' feet rested in the waters to when the waters actually stopped flowing in front of them. It took faith to do what they did.

FOOD FOR THOUGHT: I pray we are a people who want what God has for us and we are determined to possess the Promise Land. We are willing to seek God first and then step out in faith.

GOD, IT'S TOO LATE

SCRIPTURE:

Being confident of this very thing, that He who has begun a good work in you will complete it until the day of Jesus Christ. (Philippians 1:6)

We never stop growing spiritually. God is very patient in raising His children to full maturity in Him. If we think it is too late for us to change, we have placed God in a box and limited Him in helping us. We indirectly tell God that we are not willing to change. Sometimes change is very frightening. We may even suffer physically and emotionally. But if we want to reap God's best in our lives, we put ourselves on His alter and thus place our lives in His all-knowing and capable hands. Jesus said, "If anyone desires to come after Me, let him deny himself, take up his cross daily, and follow Me" (Luke 9:23).

Remember, if we are willing, God does the changing. We can't do it in our own strength. As long as we have breath, there is an opportunity to say "Yes" to God.

Remember, no sin is too great for God to forgive (except speaking against the Holy Spirit as emphasized in Matthew 12:32). We may have done something we feel so shameful about and we try to hide it from everybody, even God. We think we are protecting ourselves by not admitting to it. God is omniscient. He knows and sees all. He is just waiting for us to ask Him for His help.

We may have failed at something so many times that we can no longer count. But God tells us to never give up. Never look back at the past. Today is a new day. Each day is a fresh start to conquer whatever bondages, hindrances, or sins that ensnares us. In the end, we give God all the Glory. Hallelujah.

FOOD FOR THOUGHT: God, I personally have resisted your help in areas that I was too ashamed to share with you. But you showed me how much you loved me and that you desired my fellowship, regardless of what I had done. You waited patiently for me to call on you and to ask you to forgive me and to ask for your help. You have shown me your faithfulness by leading me into paths of righteousness. You have changed my rags to robes of righteousness. Father, I fall at your feet and say "thank you." I pray others will understand how much you love them and they will also place their lives in your hands.

PARK BENCH

SCRIPTURE:

For God so loved the world, that He gave His only begotten Son, that whoever believes in Him should not perish, but have everlasting life. (John 3:16)

I have sat under a man made light, the light pole. My bench seat has held many occupants – the old and the young, the rich and the poor, the proud and the destitute, the educated and the slow of mind, as well as people from the nations of the world.

Man's light sees the outside coverings of a person. However, under God's light all people are equal in His sight. He loves them all. Each person who has sat on my bench represents a soul God loves more than man can fathom.

I am consumed with a desire to reach the hurting people and to give them a Word from God. I wish I could be God's instrument to reveal His love.

There is a middle age man, wearing a dark, tailored suit, who visits me each morning with his usual cup of coffee. As he sits with straight posture and legs crossed, he reads the Wall Street Journal. He never speaks, but his mind is active like the mechanical parts of a clock.

My bench has been the disposal catcher of unwelcome vomit. Then the man falls on me. If I didn't catch him, he would be laying on the ground. He reeks of alcohol as he sleeps off its effects.

One night a young woman visited my bench. She looked very lonely as if she had no friends in the world. Her face was covered with bruises and she was holding on to a small suitcase as if it was all she owned. She was looking around to see if anyone was following her. In desperation she cried out, "Where to go? I have no place to hide. God, help me." After several minutes she left. Sometimes I wonder what happened to her.

There was a man dressed in jeans and a sweat-shirt, wearing construction work boots. I could hear him mumbling under his breath, "What am I going to do now? No job. How can I feed my family? We owe three months rent. They are threatening to take the car away. I am worthless – I can't take care of my family." Then I saw the gun. He gingerly turned the gun in his hands and then he placed it in his mouth. With tears running down his face, he pulled the trigger.

If only my bench could be God's hands, feet, and voice to the hurting. But I can't. People are God's messengers of the Good News.

FOOD FOR THOUGHT: Father, help us to look at the person the same way you do, with love and compassion for the lost. Help us to put aside our own agenda and be available to reach out to the hurting. Let our mouths be ready to speak your Word in love, not condemnation. Father, we are your servants. Use us today to reach the lost, which is the passion of your heart.

GOD'S HEART FOR THE LOST

SCRIPTURE:

The fruit of the righteous is a tree of life, and he who wins souls is wise. (Proverbs 11:30)

God loves us. His unfathomable love is beyond comprehension. He is a Holy God. He created man for fellowship with Him. However, man became separated from God when Adam and Eve disobediently ate the forbidden fruit from the tree of life.

All we like sheep have gone astray; we have turned, every one, to his own way; and the Lord has laid on Him [Jesus] the iniquity of us all (Isaiah 53:6).

For all have sinned and fall short of the glory of God (Romans 3:23).

For the wages of sin is death, but the gift of God is eternal life in Christ Jesus our Lord (Romans 6:23).

For God so loved the world that He gave His only begotten Son [Jesus], that whoever believes in Him should not perish but have everlasting life (John 3:16).

So if God sent His only son, Jesus, to pay the price for our sins and build a bridge between Him and us, then we should consider this a very important issue in God's heart.

If we want our heart to line up with God's heart, we must have a passion for the lost. This should be high priority in our lives.

FOOD FOR THOUGHT: Father God, forgive us for being slack in not being sensitive to the Holy Spirit when a lost soul has been placed in our path. Your Word explains we are supposed to be salt and light to the world. We have been delinquent in this call. Give us a heart that is passionate for the lost, just as your heart is.

A CHILD IS BORN

SCRIPTURE:

Let this mind be in you which was also in Christ Jesus, who, being in the form of God, did not consider it robbery to be equal with God, but made Himself of no reputation, taking the form of a bondservant, and coming in the likeness of men. (Philippians 2:5-7)

A boy child comes forth with a cry. However, this child is like no other child. The God of the universe has sent His only son to this world as a baby, who is the temple for the glory of God here on Earth. Take a moment and think about this very special child. He will do all the same daily activities as any other child, such as eating, playing, and sleeping. He will need to learn how to talk, walk, read, and write just like everyone else here on Earth. When he stumbles and falls, He will know the love of a father and mother who will take care of His bruises. As He plays and learns, He will also be in submission to parents who will guide Him on the path from childhood to manhood.

As Mary holds her son, God's son, in her arms, she is overwhelmed with the immensity of her purpose and responsibility in this life. Then the peaceful anointing of this Christ Child is transmitted to her. She knows in the deepest part of her heart that God will be with her at every step. She looks into Jesus' eyes, which shines like the stars of creation. And the joy of when Jesus laughs and giggles! There is nothing like the honesty of a child's laughter that comes forth from deep down in a bottomless well, like a fountain of living water.

Then the day comes when He is grown. He must leave the safety of home and go out into the world to fulfill His destiny. This child...this man...this Son of God will have to encounter the same trials that any human faces on Earth. The only difference is that He will walk His path with the anointing of God, the Holy Spirit, while showing us how to walk our path.

This child was sent by God to be our redeemer. The enormity of this statement: from Heaven to Earth to Heaven. The day will come when one word from Him, Jesus the Christ, will hush all the noise of civilization. The world will know that He is the One and only true Messiah. All will bow down to this man, named Jesus, who is the King of Kings and the Lord of Lords.

On Christmas day we celebrate the birth of this child, Jesus, the ultimate gift of God's love for us.

FOOD FOR THOUGHT: Jesus, thank you for choosing to come to Earth as a child, leaving your home of glory with God the Father. Just as you were willing to come, I pray that we are willing to be a vessel of your love to a lost and dying world.

NEVER TOO LATE

SCRIPTURE:

Then all the tax collectors and the sinners drew near to Him to hear Him. And the Pharisees and scribes complained, saying, "This Man receives sinners and eats with them."

So He [Jesus] spoke this parable to them, saying, "What man of you, having a hundred sheep, if he loses one of them, does not leave the ninety-nine in the wilderness, and go after the one which is lost until he finds it? And when he has found it, he lays it on his shoulders, rejoicing. And when he comes home, he calls together his friends and neighbors, saying to them, 'Rejoice with me, for I have found my sheep which was lost!' I say to you that likewise there will be more joy in heaven over one sinner who repents than over ninety-nine just persons who need no repentance." (Luke 15:1-7)

Henry, at the age of seventy-two, had already served twenty-five years in prison. He was a resident of death row in more ways than one. The doctors stated it was a matter of weeks, or maybe even days, before his cancer-ridden body would give up the fight to live. Henry was a bitter and angry man, whose spoken words were venomous like a snake. The blasphemous, unspeakable words that continuously left his mouth matched his temper. No one in the infirmary wanted to treat him.

There was a young Chaplin by the name of Joseph who determined in his heart he would reach Henry with the gospel before it was too late. The first day that Joseph went to see Henry, he was met with cursing and resistance. Henry would have nothing to do with Joseph and the message he brought.

Joseph was not deterred by the obscene language. He understood that Satan was the author of all this hate. Joseph responded, "I love you and God loves you." Then Joseph walked out.

The next day when Joseph visited Henry, he was met with, "I thought I told you to get out and never come back."

At that moment Henry began to cough, so Joseph brought him a glass of water. Henry slapped Joseph's hand and between bouts of coughing told Joseph to get out. However, Joseph obtained another glass of water. Again Henry slapped the glass out of Joseph's hand. This continued until Henry was too weak to resist. The male nurse asked if he should intervene, but Joseph waved the man away. Joseph gently pressed the glass of water to Henry's lips. This time Henry was unable to fight Joseph. Some of the water was able to wet his lips and slither down his throat. When Joseph was done, he left the room with these words, "I love you and God loves you."

The more Joseph tried to be nice to him, Henry grew meaner. Henry was determined. Each day Joseph visited Henry with kind words and deeds. Joseph never became frustrated. Every time that

Henry would curse him, Joseph would respond, "I love you and God loves you."

After about ten days of this engaging battle, Henry asked, "How can God love a scoundrel and a murderer like me? I have blasphemed God ever since I was a child. Never once have I met anyone demonstrate love the way you have."

Joseph responded, "God loves you so much that He sent His only son, Jesus, to die on the cross for you. Every kind of sin was placed on Jesus. God did not pick and choose certain sins.

All sin was placed on Jesus. Even though Jesus never sinned, He received the punishment for all of mankind's sins. The shed blood of Jesus wiped the slate clean, so that man can spend eternity with God in Heaven. It is like trading your punishment for freedom. God is waiting for you with open arms to receive you at your last breath. All you have to do is choose Jesus. It is never too late to ask Jesus to forgive you. The alternative is Hell (the place set apart for Satan and his cohorts) where there is eternity of torment. God does not send a person there. You choose to go there by rejecting His son, Jesus."

Henry was quiet for a long time. Then he asked Joseph, "Why did you show kindness to me even though I continued to be hateful to you?"

"God showed me the only way to destroy hate is by letting love be bigger than the hate."

"I have known hate all my life. I am tired. I want to know the love you have."

Joseph proceeded to lead Henry in the sinner's prayer.

The next day when Joseph came to visit, Henry was unconscious. Joseph was pleased to see that Henry's countenance was different. His face was relaxed with a slight smile that seeped through the closed lips. As Joseph reached over to hold Henry's hand, he heard Henry's last breath as he passed from this world to the next.

(This story is based on a true story I heard many years ago.)

FOOD FOR THOUGHT: Help us to remember that you love those who don't know you and who hate you, even those who have done incomprehensible things in life. You came to this Earth to find the lost sheep and bring them back home to you. You don't want anyone to perish. It is never too late, so let us never give up praying for the lost.

FIRST LOVE

SCRIPTURE:

Nevertheless I have this against you, that you have left your first love. (Revelation 2:4)

I met Him yesterday. I couldn't think of anything or anyone else. All I could do was look at the One who had captured my heart. I was mesmerized by every word that came from His mouth. I was in awe of the power of His words. I could even feel the strength of His countenance. These feelings of love were new to me. My whole being felt alive, like nothing I have ever felt before. This was all because of Him. He looked at me. My heart skipped a beat. Can this possibly be real? Is He calling me to follow Him?

Later that day, I tried to eat, but food had no interest for me. I wondered if I would see Him again. There was such power and confidence in His words. It seemed that nothing could over power Him. And, Oh! That look! I saw eyes full of love, compassion, and mercy. He had touched my heart. I would never be the same again.

That night I tried to go to sleep, but my mind was alert with the memory of Him. I had never met anyone like Him. The butterflies did a dance in my stomach. My brain was like a computer that I could not turn off. Sleep evaded me.

Today, I knew I wanted to see Him again. My mind reviewed over and over again our first encounter. I counted the minutes; yet, time seemed to stand still. My heart was filled with the longing of being in His presence. I finally arrived at my destination. I excitedly looked for Him; but I didn't see Him. I panicked. I have to see Him. I need to see Him. I cannot live without Him.

I cried out with a loud, desperate voice, "Did you see which way He went?"

Then I heard Him call my name. With stammering lips and tears in my eyes, I answered, "Here I am."

I turned and He was there. He gently said, "I will never leave you. All you need to do is call my name and I am here."

My heart was so full I thought it would burst. "Jesus, I love you more than words can say."

FOOD FOR THOUGHT: My prayer is that we will return to our first love, when our heart was totally surrendered to Him. We felt like we were walking on air, so free from bondages and snares of this life. We had found precious gold – Jesus.

THE WALTZ

SCRIPTURE:

For your Maker is your husband. The Lord of hosts is His name; and your Redeemer is the Holy One of Israel; He is called the God of the whole earth. (Isaiah 54:5)

As the music plays, the prince approaches the woman, adorned in a long white gown. He gracefully, but eagerly reaches out to her with his left hand; she gently lays her soft, right hand into his sturdy, strong hand. He reaches around her waist with his right arm, tenderly pulling her to him. In response, she places her right hand on his broad shoulder. Slowly, in harmony with the melody of the Viennese Waltz, the prince leads his bride around the ballroom floor. As she relaxes in the security of his embrace, she forgets the world around her, totally enraptured by the one she has given her heart to. They gaze into each other's eyes. Without words, their eyes speak of the love they have for each other and no one else. The onlookers are swept away with the couple, who is gliding across the floor as one...the gracefulness, the intimacy, the unity.

The waltz is usually the first dance after a wedding, when the bride and groom have been joined together as one flesh. The Bible says that we are the bride of Christ and we are anxiously looking ahead to the day of the marriage supper of the Lamb.

In my imagination, I have enjoyed the Waltz... As I look into the compassionate and loving eyes of Jesus, I am drawn closer into His presence. When I place my hand into his strong and sturdy hands, I am entrusting my life into His sovereign wisdom. As He leads, I follow, knowing I am safe in His arms of protection. As we waltz through life, I know that Jesus will always be by my side. The soothing music of the Waltz reminds me of the peace of Jesus that covers all the storms of life.

I am the bride of Christ (see Isaiah 61:9-10).

FOOD FOR THOUGHT: In my moments of worship, I imagine myself waltzing with an invisible partner, my heart totally given over to the One and Only – Jesus. There will come a day when I will see Him face to face. Until then, in the moments of the Waltz, I sense the protection and love of my Lord and Savior. As the world watches me, I pray they will see the passion I have for my Savior.

FROM THE GARDEN

In the garden I can feel you,
Loving Spirit sent to me;
That's your bidding,
Gentle breezes calling sinners unto
Thee.

In the garden I can hear you,
Sending notes to me alone;
That's your message,
Oh so tender,
How I long to be your own.

In the garden I can taste you,
Nursed on milk of Holy Truth;
That's your Word so freely given,
Sent to reap abundant fruit.

In the garden I can smell
Your dew-splashed fragrance
Sweet and pure;
That's your essence sent to hold me,
As my arm reaches out to yours.

In the garden I can see you,
Purest white beyond compare;
That's your image meant to challenge,
Till I meet you in the air.

In the world there is a calling,
From the garden I must go;
That's my duty,
Boldly telling of the
Christ who loves me so.

By Ron Massman

GARMENTS THAT WE WEAR

SCRIPTURE:

Love covers all sins. (Proverbs 10:12b)

The general opinion is that clothes depict a person. If we see a person dressed in rags, we automatically assume that person is poor; however, if that person is dressed in diamonds and expensive clothes, we assume he is rich. The Word of God is filled with scriptures of various types of garments we wear. Some garments portray *positive* connotations, such as:

He who overcomes shall be clothed in white garments (Revelation 3:5).

Be clothed with humility (1 Peter 5:5).

Strength and honor are her clothing (Proverbs 31:25).

Put on the whole armor of God, that you may be able to stand against the wiles of the devil (Ephesians 6:11).

Then there are garments that have *negative* connotations:

He clothed himself with cursing as with his garment (Psalm 109:18).

Shame has covered my face (Psalm 69:7).

Pride serves as their necklace; violence covers them like a garment (Psalm 73:6).

Drowsiness will clothe a man with rags (Proverbs 23:21).

In addition to the above, consider these garments:

Let your priests, O lord God, be clothed with salvation (2 Chronicles 6:41).

She took off her widow's garments... (Genesis 38:14).

Jehoiachin changed from his prison garments (2 Kings 25:29, Jeremiah 52:33).

They brought him [Joseph] quickly out of the dungeon; and he shaved, changed his clothing [prison garments] and came to Pharaoh (Genesis 41:14).

Clothed with foreign apparel (Zephaniah 1:8).

Throughout life we wear various garments, both physically and spiritually. When people look at us, which garments do they see? Are they garments of pride, envy, hatred, jealousy, anger, drunkenness; or are they garments of love, humility, righteousness, peace, joy? God has asked us to put away the foreign gods that are among us, to purify ourselves, and change our garments (see Genesis 35:2). May we change our prison garments of sin and put on the garments of righteousness? Just imagine standing before the throne and before the Lamb, clothed with white robes (see Revelation 7:9). If we choose Jesus as our Savior, these will be our eternal garments. We are now clothed with earthly bodies which are mortal, but we earnestly desire to be clothed with our heavenly bodies, which are eternal (see 2 Corinthians 5:2).

One last thought to consider – Moses' face shone after he had been in the presence of God (see Exodus 34:29). When people look at us, can they tell by our countenance if we have been in the presence of God?

FOOD FOR THOUGHT: Father, I pray that when the world looks at me, they can tell by my countenance and my spiritual garments that I have been in the presence of God.

SOLDIER IN THE ARMY OF GOD

SCRIPTURE:

Now then, we are ambassadors for Christ, as though God were pleading through us: we implore you on Christ's behalf, be reconciled to God. (2 Corinthians 5:20)

My husband, Glenn, was a soldier in the Army for eight years active and the remaining years in the National Guard Reserves. When he wore his uniform with the shiny medals, I was proud of him and what he represented. I would get a lump in my throat and tears would well up in my eyes. Before he died, Glenn asked to be buried in his skivvies, not the dress uniform. He emphatically declared, "I want to be dressed in the same uniform as the men who lost their lives on the field of battle."

When God looks at His children, He sees Jesus and His blood that covers us with a white robe of righteousness. Who could ask for a more excellent uniform? Just as I was proud of Glenn, God is proud of us, actually even greater because God's love is pure and holy.

We have been given a wonderful gift from God, salvation and freedom from eternity in hell. In turn, we want to share the gift to a lost and dying world. In so doing we become ambassadors for God, or in other words, soldiers in the army of God.

On Earth, soldiers receive medals for acts of service to our country. In Heaven, we receive a crown for doing God's work ministering to others.

As we complete the Great Commission (Matthew 28:18-20) here on Earth, God gives us the weapons we need to win: the Word of God, the Blood of Jesus, and the Holy Spirit.

GREAT COMMISSION: Jesus came and spoke to them, saying, "All authority has been given to Me in heaven and in earth. Go therefore and make disciples of all the nations, baptizing them in the name of the Father and of the Son and of the Holy Spirit, teaching them to observe all things that I have commanded you; and lo, I am with you always, even to the end of the age" (Matthew 28:18-20).

Let us be obedient to the command of our heavenly Commander in Chief. As a soldier of God, we have an enemy, Satan. But the Bible reminds us that Satan is a defeated foe. We have read the end of the book and it says that we win.

FOOD FOR THOUGHT: We are soldiers in the army of God, fighting Satan. We are seeking the captives and bringing freedom from bondage to those who are bound by Satan's deceitful tactics. Our weapons are God's Word and His love. The last chapter of the Bible foretells our victory.

ARMOR OF GOD

SCRIPTURE:

Put on the whole armor of God, that you may be able to stand against the wiles of the devil. (Ephesians 6:11)

No devotion to God would be complete without preparing for the battles ahead. For certainly the enemy is ready and waiting, be it from without or within. Dawn proudly the Armor of God each and every morning.

Helmet of Salvation: If we have admitted that we are a sinner, asked Jesus to forgive us of our sins, and made Him Lord of our lives, then we can put on the helmet of salvation. This piece of armor is our covering and protection over our lives and minds as we walk with God and stand against the enemy, Satan.

Breastplate of Righteousness: The Blood of Jesus covers and protects our heart and lungs, our life giving organs, which flow with blood and oxygen. When God looks at us, He does not see our sins that have been washed away forever by the Blood of Jesus. He sees the righteousness of Jesus. Even in battle, the enemy sees this breastplate of righteousness and knows that Jesus is on our side.

Loins Girded with Truth: According to *Webster Dictionary*, loins are the hips and lower abdomen regarded as the region of strength. It is also the area covering the reproductive region. By knowing the truth about who we are in Christ Jesus, we have weapons that will help us to stand against the enemy.

Sword of the Spirit: This weapon is the living Word of God. As the Word is spoken out of our mouths, its creative power is released. As we put the Word in our hearts, our faith is built up. Also, as a child of God, we have the mind of Christ. We learn to think like Him by renewing our minds daily with the Word of God.

Shield of Faith: As previously inferred, faith comes from hearing the Word of God. As we load our quiver with the Word and speak its creative power against the enemy, our faith in God's Word and Christ blocks his fiery darts.

Feet Shod with the Preparation of the Gospel of Peace: We are soldiers for Christ. Everywhere we walk is holy ground. We are prepared each day to be a vessel for God, releasing His provision to a lost and dying world.

FOOD FOR THOUGHT: Each part of this armor is connected and needed to stand against Satan, and his evil cohorts. Daily we need to pray and study the Word to receive the protection this armor provides.

PEACE OF GOD

SCRIPTURES:

And the peace of God, which surpasses all understanding, will guard your hearts and minds through Christ Jesus. (Philippians 4:7)

Peace I leave with you, My peace I give to you; not as the world gives do I give to you. Let not your heart be troubled, neither let it be afraid. (John 14:27)

When God speaks, peace fills my heart. His voice quiets the rampaging voices. His voice, His Word spoken to me, brings a "stillness", as if time stands still. In that moment when peace washes over me, I feel secure in Him.

I have a friend, Mary, who has prayed with me many times when I have faced some mighty trials of life. My head and heart were in turmoil. As she prayed the Word of God over me, I actually felt the peace of God cover me like a warm blanket. At that moment, I knew God could handle anything.

When we lay our problems at the feet of Jesus and trust Him, peace enters our hearts and gives us faith that helps us to walk through the valleys.

Peace is a weapon in our arsenal. We are able to accomplish much more if we let peace control the situation, instead of our flesh. A kind word can tear down walls, but a harsh word can build them up.

In the early years of my marriage, I displayed my temper with loud, angry words. All it accomplished was my husband shutting down and not talking. I later learned that when I spoke to him with "non-yelling" words, he was more ready to listen.

If you want peace in your life, be willing to plant the seed of peace. In the beatitudes Jesus states, "Blessed are the peacemakers, for they shall be called the sons of God" (Matthew 5:9). Nothing compares to the peace of God. It cannot be re-created by man. The only way to know the peace of God is to know Him as Lord.

FOOD FOR THOUGHT: Father, we seek the peace of God, which surpasses all understanding that will guard our hearts against the storms of life.

YOU MUST PAINT YOUR HOUSE

SCRIPTURE:

But I discipline my body and bring it into subjection, lest, when I have preached to others, I myself should become disqualified. (1 Corinthians 9:27)

As I was walking on the treadmill one day, God gave me the title "You must paint your house." I asked him, "I thought you looked at the heart, not the outward appearance." He went on to remind me that He was referring to the health of our bodies.

When you live in a house there are upkeeps we must do in order to keep the house in running condition; such as, repairing broken windows, fixing electrical fixtures and pipes, mowing the lawns, caulking around the windows to keep the hot or cold air outside, and even painting the outside of the house when the paint starts flaking.

The same is true for the physical bodies we live in. We must take care of the inside and the outside of this house, so that we can be in tip-top condition for fulfilling our destiny. If we become overweight, our endurance is compromised. If we are addicted to cigarettes, sugar, alcohol, or drugs, we could be shortening our life span. God wants our bodies disciplined so we can run our race with endurance.

Life is filled with many reasons that tempt us to indulge in those areas of weakness that have bound us. That is what the devil wants. He wants our bodies to deteriorate physically so that we are unable to be productive in our service for God.

We all may have areas that we struggle in. If you don't, be very thankful. If we are serious about following after God, we must learn how to discipline our bodies so they are healthy. If we need to lose weight, we need to watch what we eat and exercise. If we smoke, we need to find a way to quit. The same goes for any addictions we have.

What is great in this whole matter is that we have the Holy Spirit that will help us. According to Philippians 4:13, I can do all things through Christ who strengthens me. Take one day at a time. Each day is a new day. So if we messed up yesterday, we can start afresh today. Never give up. Then one day we will realize that we have succeeded in our struggle.

FOOD FOR THOUGHT: Father, we ask for your help in breaking the addictions in our lives. As we discipline our bodies, we need to forgive ourselves when we slip up and not let it keep us from going forward in the process. With determination as of a champion, we keep at it until we have won the race.

SHOPPING FOR GOD

SCRIPTURE:

I charge you therefore before God and the Lord Jesus Christ, who will judge the living and the dead at His appearing and His kingdom: Preach the word! Be ready in season and out of season. Convince, rebuke, exhort, with all longsuffering and teaching. For the time will come when they will not endure sound doctrine, but according to their own desires, because they have *itching ears*, they will heap up for themselves teachers; and they will turn their ears away from the truth, and be turned aside to fables. (2 Timothy 4:1-4)

The Bible forewarns us that in the latter days we need to guard our minds and be careful what we allow in. The airways are exploding with information, some line up with the Word of God, while others do not. If we do not know what the Word says, then we do not know whether the information is incorrect or not. We need to be very careful we are not drawn away from the truth by things that sound good. If it doesn't agree with God's Word, we must not let ourselves be persuaded or seduced by false doctrines. This is what God is referring to when he tells us to beware of itching ears.

"This is the 90's" is a common phrase people speak to delude themselves to think God's Word is not for today. People tend to shop for churches that will allow them to live in their sin. Instead of changing their lives to line up with the Word of God, they want to change the Word to line up with their lives. If we want to live a holy and pure life that is filled with the anointing power of God, we must know what God's Word says regarding certain subjects. The Bible holds the answer to every single problem we face.

Some people may feel intimidated by the Bible, thinking they are unable to understand what the written word says. There was a time in history when we were told we could not read the Bible. The theologians believed ordinary people were unable to comprehend the Word of God. But we have the Holy Spirit who desires to reveal to us what God wants to say to us through the Bible. Before we read a passage, we can ask the Holy Spirit to help us.

Instead of shopping around for people or churches that will satisfy our "itching ears," let's open the Good Book – the Bible. It is the handbook for life.

FOOD FOR THOUGHT: My heart's cry is that I am not led astray by false doctrine. I pray I will be willing to line up what people say with the Word of God, and choose the latter as the final authority on the subject.

A DATE WITH GOD

SCRIPTURES:

Behold, I stand at the door and knock. If anyone hears My voice and opens the door, I will come in to him and dine with him, and he with Me. (Revelation 3:20)

Noah walked with God. (Genesis 6:9)

Now before him [Josiah] there was no king like him, who turned to the Lord with all his heart, with all his soul, and with all his might, according to the Law of Moses. (2 Kings 23:25)

When my husband passed away, there were times I felt so alone. When I saw other couples together in a restaurant, I was reminded of what I no longer had. When I returned from work to an empty house, the walls would close in on me. The silence was deafening. When I laid my head down at night to go to sleep, I felt the emptiness of the bed.

Then one day a thought came to me. I was going to have a date with God. I grabbed my Bible and a pad of paper. I drove to a local restaurant. When I walked in, I chose a quiet table in the corner of the establishment so that I could be alone with God. I read. I ate. I prayed. I ate. I read. I ate. I wrote down words God dropped into my spirit. When I was full, both of food and comfort, I said thank you to God, and I went home. I knew in my heart I would need to make this a regular outing.

Since then I have found several occasions to have a date with God. Sometimes I have gone to a local park early in the morning. I would sit on a swing and talk with God. I lifted up the praises in my heart for the things He has brought me through. As God talked to me, I felt He had taken time for me.

When I am driving my car, I have the radio tabbed to a Christian radio station. As I listen to the songs, God and I have special moments together.

I have even thought of going to a movie that both God and I would enjoy. We could talk about the movie and that we enjoyed the time we spent together, especially since I chose the number one person in the universe to go with.

Many times during the day, I find myself talking to God about the little things, such as the enjoyment of my four year old granddaughter's expression of life.

Some people may think it is unusual talking to God like this. Why not? He wants us to talk to Him in our daily lives. He is just as real as anyone else. I look forward to those times I go to the restaurant or to the park. I enjoy the times I spend with Him. At those times, God reassures me that I am not alone.

FOOD FOR THOUGHT: God, I pray we will never stop taking time out to have a date with you. I pray we will realize that you get excited when we do this.

I pray our imaginations will run wild with ideas of how to spend time with you. A date with the God of the Universe is greater than prom night, meeting the President of the United States, our wedding day, or the birth of our baby.

CHILD OF GOD

SCRIPTURE:

But those who seek the Lord shall not lack any good thing. (Psalm 34:10)

I am a child of God. Abba Father, the creator of the universe, watches over me and protects me from the snares of the devil, the evil one who desires to destroy me and keep me away from God.

I walk in the light of God's wisdom. He has prepared a table of blessings for me. He is with me when I walk through the valleys of life. He is with me when I stand on the mountain top and declare His victories. My heavenly Father and I spend time daily talking to each other. He takes pleasure in me. He enjoys the fact I share my day with Him. I sing praises to the One who adorns me with good gifts. If I am obedient to His statutes, He has promised blessings beyond my imagination. He declares He never leaves me and nothing can stop His love for me. He is my counselor, my comforter, my helper, my deliverer, my shelter from the enemy, and my strong tower of defense.

I wake up each morning knowing it will be a great day, because the Lord God is on my side. I have the authority and power to tell Satan to leave and not bother me. My thoughts are filled with good things – hope of a future that will be spent in eternity with God in Heaven. Depression is no longer my bedfellow. I have a sound mind that is focused on the things of God. I don't need the vices of cigarettes, alcohol, or food to help me through the day. My strength comes from Him who brings purpose in my life.

I enjoy fellowshipping with my brothers and sisters in Christ. My "high' is being in His presence. When I talk to others about the things of God, I invite His presence in our conversations.

I can lay my burdens down. God wants me to give my cares and worries to Him. He is better equipped to solve the problems. While He is taking care of the problems in my life, I am free to enjoy each day. When I go to bed at the end of the day, my sleep is filled with sweet dreams. I am not afraid of tomorrow, because I know He has gone before me and He has prepared a way for me. I rest in Him, knowing He is the One who carries me through the storm. Nothing compares to my God. He is my everything.

FOOD FOR THOUGHT: I pray people will understand that there is an actual difference between life with God and life without Him. I pray they will desire to live in my world. All they have to do is say "Yes" to Jesus and they too can become a child of God.

TREE OF PAIN

So tall and full I stood that day,
A king among the stand I may;
Strong limbs spread out for shade and nest,
Lest beast or fowl come near for rest.

But now I stand, my blood long dried,
Deserted, stripped and bare of hide;
Once proud, my countenance now shows,
The wretched tool of pain men chose.

Again this day I clutch a man,
Hung high with spikes in foot and hand;
In times like these I feel that dread,
His fate like mine: As good as dead!

Somehow I sense a different air,
This man of woe, He really cares!
Thus beaten, scourged and brought down low,
He then forgives them all their blows!

My loss was not gain, his was not defeat.
The blood that runs down to their feet
Has soaked this dry and parched shell,
Renewed and proud: His message tell!

Like Him, in silence came I neigh.
For Him, a shameful place to die.
To Him, a King's stark irony.
By Him, my place I plainly see!

As Stones cry out their praises still,
'Till all the sparrows sing their fill,
I'll trust my Maker's holy prayer,
My seed: 'Tis His to sow up there!

By Ron Massman

TREE OF LIFE

Hear, oh man, of time and space,
A thought thy mind to weave;
A message frot with visions rare,
A hope thy soul to cleave.

Winding through this land
On high a river flows for thee;
Thus gaining speed by love's design,
Downstream thy destiny.

Rooted deep 'neath soil above
My nourishment conceives,
A canopy for thou to share
With all who do believe.

Adorned with fruit of living stock
Thy needs wilt be supplied;
Then uncorrupted, evermore,
In HIM thou wilt abide!

The joy of love that knows no bounds
Thou now do vaguely see;
Set free that day to be unveiled,
Thy FATHER'S will conceived.

To me flow thoughts of long ago;
Misused and ill applied,
A tree of pain I was 'till death;
Brought now back by HIS side!

These songs of praise I envy not:
Nor prayers designed to soar
With incense sweet with
The redeemed to HIM forevermore!

So, of a truth, who can but say
These visions thou do see;
We both can share,
We both can claim to LIFE and VICTORY!

By Ron Massman

GOD CAN USE ORDINARY PEOPLE

SCRIPTURE:

But the Lord said to Samuel, "Do not look at his appearance or at his physical stature, because I have refused him. For the Lord does not see as man sees; for man looks at the outward appearance, but the Lord looks at the heart." (1 Samuel 16:7)

Lord, I am nobody. I am shy. I am not very smart. I am not beautiful. I stutter. I don't have a lot of money. I have a past of sin. God, why would you want to use someone like me?

As I read the Bible, God has shown me that He uses ordinary people to accomplish His purpose here on Earth. Even some of the men in the Bible, whom we thought were great, have had their areas of sin.

Abraham is listed in the Bible as the Father of faith; however, he was a liar. When Abraham and his wife, Sarah, were in Egypt, he told Pharaoh that Sarah was his sister (see Genesis 12:13).

Moses, who led the Israelites out of Egypt, was a murderer (see Exodus 2:12). Moses even told God that he was "slow of speech" and asked God to send someone else (see Exodus 4:10, 13).

David was a shepherd boy, whom God chose to be King; however, King David was an adulterer and a murderer. He slept with Bathsheba, the wife of

Uriah. Then David had Uriah killed (see 2 Samuel 11).

Gideon told God, "How can I save Israel? Indeed my clan is the weakest in Manasseh, and I am the least in my father's house" (Judges 6:15). God used Gideon to defeat the Midianites who were oppressing Israel.

Rahab, the harlot, was NOT an Israelite; but she chose to help them when she hid the three Israelite spies from the men of Jericho (see Joshua 2). What excited me when I read about Rahab was that Rahab is listed in the genealogy of Jesus. "Salmon begot Boaz by *Rahab*, Boaz begot Obed by Ruth, Obed begot Jesse, and Jesse begot David the king...." (Matthew 1:5, 6).

I even read about Peter, the fisherman, who walked with Jesus. Peter denied Jesus three times (see Matthew 26:69-75). Later I read how Peter became a mighty spokesman for Jesus.

The list goes on and on. Our response to God should be, "Here I am Lord, use me."

FOOD FOR THOUGHT: Father, I am grateful the Bible shows that you can use ordinary people. I don't have to be perfect. All I have to do is have a heart that follows after you and is available. Father, as we place our lives in your hands, use us.

A PARTY

SCRIPTURE:

The kingdom of heaven is like a certain king who arranged a marriage for his son, and sent out his servants to call those who were invited to the wedding; and they were not willing to come. (Matthew 22:2-3)

In a large room that is filled with many people are guest who have been invited by God to this party. The guests include three major groups.

The *first group* are those who are wandering around the outskirts of the room. They stay as far away as possible from entering into what is happening in the middle. They may take a glance, but they avoid the honored speaker.

The *second group* is closer. They have met the speaker and want to have an intimate conversation; however, they don't try to navigate their way into the center of the room where the speaker is.

The *third group* works to get as close to the speaker as possible. They linger on his every word. Their sole purpose is to fellowship with him.

Who is the main speaker? *Jesus.*

The group closest to Jesus spends personal time with Him regularly and frequently.

The middle group knows and loves Jesus, but their busy lives sometimes keep them from having an intimate relationship with Him.

The group on the outskirts has not decided whether to stay or leave. They are the ones who are on the fence and have not made a decision to know Jesus, the bruises of this life having kept them away.

In which group do you belong?

FOOD FOR THOUGHT: For those who are in the group close to Jesus, I pray they will continue to always put Him first in their lives. For those who are in the middle group, I pray they will realize the importance of putting Jesus first and do whatever is necessary to have that intimate fellowship. For those who are on the outskirts, I ask God to do whatever is necessary to heal their hearts and draw them close to Jesus so they can know Him personally.

I AM THE CLAY, YOU ARE THE POTTER

SCRIPTURES:

But now, O Lord, You are our Father; we are the clay, and You our potter; and all we are the work of Your hand. (Isaiah 64:8)

"O house of Israel, can I not do with you as this potter?" says the Lord. "Look, as the clay is in the potter's hand, so are you in My hand, O house of Israel!" (Jeremiah 18:6)

My child, I have a message to give to you. You see yourself as an ugly vase covered in mud with sharp pebbles protruding from the surface. Hiding behind this wall of mud, you do not allow anyone to look inside. You believe that if anyone saw inside they would confirm that you have no value.

My child, I have something to tell you. When I look at you, I see a beautiful, multi-faceted, brilliant-colored vase. My desire is that you would see what I see in you.

Step unto the potter's wheel. Put your trust into my precise hands that can create a masterpiece without causing any damage. I know how to remove the stones and pebbles that are embedded in the mud. Let me wash the mud off and smooth the rough edges.

When I have finished polishing, the light that is on the inside of you will shine through. The world will be able to see the beautiful vessel that I can see. You will be a witness of the handiwork of God. Your light will shine forth and touch others with the beauty that I see.

FOOD FOR THOUGHT: Father, you have created me. I step unto the potter's wheel. I trust my life in your hands. Do whatever is needed to bring out that beautiful vase that you see.

GUILT FREE

SCRIPTURE:

For as the heavens are high above the Earth, so great is His mercy toward those who fear Him; as far as the east is from the west, so far has He removed our transgressions from us. (Psalm 103:11, 12)

I once was a sinner, separated from the presence of God. I chose the path of pride and rebellion, instead of the truth of God's Word. The consequences of my sinful choices brought shame and guilt. I wore them like an anchor around my neck, unable to break free.

But because of an encounter with Jesus, I learned to walk a new path. I was told I was forgiven and cleansed by the blood of Jesus; my sins were washed away, never to be remembered again by God.

Just as darkness and light are opposites, Sin and a Holy God don't correlate. At the cross Jesus paid the penalty for man's disobedience. He provided a way so we could enter into the presence of God.

On my new path, I discovered I still tried to drag along the weight of guilt. I had become so familiar with its companionship, like a comforter wrapped around me. Then one day, God reminded me I no longer had to carry the guilt. I can walk guilt free – one of the benefits of the blood that eradicated my sins.

Yes, Jesus paid the price so I could be totally free from the bondage of sin. Now I need to learn to accept the fullness of all that Jesus has done for me. I am allowed to walk in forgiveness, with my past behind me. It will no longer have a grip on my future.

FOOD FOR THOUGHT: We can understand that God has forgiven us; but so many times we never learn to forgive ourselves. We allow the guilt to be like a film on the mirror, not allowing us to see God clearly. As they say, "Been there, done that. I have worn the T-shirt." Father, we place the guilt of our past at your feet. Help us to forgive ourselves.

SANCTIFY ME, O LORD

SCRIPTURES:

Blessed are the pure in heart, for they shall see God. (Matthew 5:8)

Search me, O God, and know my heart; try me, and know my anxieties; and see if there is any wicked way in me, and lead me in the way everlasting. (Psalm 139:23-24)

Just as King David cried out to a Holy and merciful God, I also fall on my face before you and beseech you to search my heart. Go deep with your delicate surgeon's hands into all the intricate places. When you are done, I am confident there will be no scars.

You have eyes that can see in the deepest and darkest places that have been even hidden from my conscious mind. There are bruises and injuries that have been pushed down into these crevices of darkness, because I have been unable to handle the overload of the pain. They are like hidden aneurysms (sacs formed by an enlargement in a weakened wall of an artery, vein, or heart) that could surface at any time and cause damage. Only you know the ultimate solution that will wipe away the affects of a bruised heart.

While you are doing this intricate open-heart surgery, I also ask you to remove the dark plaque of sins that are rampaging and clogging the arteries of my heart. Open up all the passages so that life can flow freely again. When you have completed your masterful surgery, there will be no cancerous spots left on the X-ray. Only a pure heart.

FOOD FOR THOUGHT: Lord, shine your light on my heart and search all the hidden corners, even where the cobwebs cover hidden hurts or secret sins. If there is anything you see that does not please you, I give you permission to draw it out. Heal my heart and make me whole again.

I FAILED, EXCEPT FOR
THE GRACE OF GOD

SCRIPTURE:

For by grace you have been saved through faith, and that not of yourselves: it is the gift of God, not of works, lest anyone should boast. (Ephesians 2:8, 9)

When I was young, I did not betray the truth that was taught me in church. My claims to victory included: A-B honor roll, accepted at a major university, "sweet sixteen and never been kissed", never smoked, never did drugs, and never drank. My past was clean. My future was filled with promises.

What happened? The glitter and limelight of the world, the "forbidden fruit" that God said we should not eat, the life that was intriguing and dangerous lured me away from my clean slate to committing the sins that darkened my soul.

I so wanted to be that person that could say that I grew up in church, I stayed in church, and I am still in church. But I can't say that. I wanted to be able to say that I never tasted the lusts of the flesh. But I can't say that. I wanted to show the straight A's that I made with each challenge of life. But I can't do that. I will never be able to do that.

But, I can say, "Jesus". That name alone (not works) will allow me to stand before God and say that my slate is clean. Because of the blood of Jesus, my sins have been washed away, never to be remembered again. The blood of Jesus has made me white as snow.

FOOD FOR THOUGHT: Father God, when the enemy reminds me of my past, I will remember that I can stand before you with a clean slate – the blood of Jesus has wiped away my past.

GOD LIVING IN US

SCRIPTURE:

Now we have received, not the spirit of the world, but the Spirit who is from God, that we might know the things that have been freely given to us by God. (1 Corinthians 2:12)

Recently I heard someone make a statement that spoke to my heart. He asked, "Can God live comfortably in us?" This led me to ponder on the following thoughts.

As a born again Christian we have the Holy Spirit indwelling in us. He goes everywhere we go. Would God the Holy Spirit be comfortable going to some of the places we go? He hears everything we say. Would God the Holy Spirit be embarrassed by some of the things we say? He sees everything we see. If we realized God was seeing what we were looking at, would we turn our heads away?

Are we mindful of God in our daily lives? Is God a strong abiding presence we acknowledge in everything we do? Or do we go about doing our thing, ignoring that God is in the picture?

When we walk into our days, there should be two of us: our physical bodies and the Holy Spirit that lives in us. Even though our physical bodies are visible to the people around us, it should not be dominant over the Holy Spirit. We should allow the Holy Spirit to lead us, teach us, and draw us closer to the things that please God. The way we do this is by inviting (asking) the Holy Spirit each morning to have control of our lives. We give place to His wisdom, His authority and His knowledge. We submit to His still small voice that speaks to us. He wants to be part of our daily lives, but He is a gentleman, so He won't push His way into our lives unless we ask Him. With the help of the Holy Spirit, God would be able to say that He can live comfortably in us.

FOOD FOR THOUGHT: When we wake up each morning, I pray we will ask the Holy Spirit to help us through that day. As we listen and obey that still small voice in our heart, He will help us to become more like Jesus. If we are doing something that is not pleasing to God, where God would not live comfortably in us, we should be quick to turn away from those things that displease God.

BY FAITH

SCRIPTURES:

Now faith is the substance of things hoped for, the evidence of thins not seen...But without faith it is impossible to please Him, for he who comes to God must believe that He is, and that He is a rewarder of those who diligently seek Him. (Hebrews 11:1, 6)

So then faith comes by hearing, and hearing by the Word of God. (Romans 10:17)

By faith, when I close my eyes at night, I go to sleep believing I will wake up in the morning.

By faith, my heart beats without any effort on my part. Each organ follows the direction of God's plan of creation.

By faith, I know that each breath I take comes from God.

By faith, my body has the God given nature to heal itself.

By faith, I take a step, expecting to walk forward.

By faith, the sun rises each morning and the Earth rotates around the sun.

By faith, when I drop an object it will fall to the ground.

By faith, when I hold in my arms a newborn child who is so beautiful and intricate, I know there has to be a God.

By faith, I believe that God is the author of all creation.

By faith, I believe in God, Jesus, and the Holy Spirit. I also believe in Heaven and hell, angels and demons, even though I can't see them.

By faith, God is a blink of reality beside me. Even though I am unable to see Him, He is there.

By faith, my sins are forgiven and I am washed white as snow by the blood of Jesus Christ.

By faith, the Holy Spirit lives in me to help guide me through each day.

By faith, I know my path is directed by God. He is always with me; I am never alone.

Only faith pleases God. I take no provision for the flesh to control my life.

FOOD FOR THOUGHT: There are times our faith is strong; while at other times our faith seems to be nonexistent. Father, forgive our unbelief. We determine to consistently read and learn the Word of God, so that our faith will be strong and the storms of life cannot knock us down.

DON'T LET MEN STEAL
YOUR GOD GIVEN DREAMS

SCRIPTURE:

Your Word I have hidden in my heart, that I might not sin against You. (Psalm 119:11)

The following story is narrated in 1 Kings 11 through 13. When Solomon died, the kingdom was divided, just like God had foretold to King Solomon. Rehoboam, son of Solomon, was king over the children of Israel who lived in the cities of Judah, while Jeroboam was king over the remaining tribes of the Israelites. Jeroboam was afraid that if the people went to Jerusalem to offer up sacrifices to the Lord, they may return their loyalty to Rehoboam. So Jeroboam made two calves of gold and placed them in Bethel and Dan. He made shrines on the high places and the Israelites worshiped these gods, which made God angry at Jeroboam because he had caused the children of God to sin.

A man of God cried out against these altars. He declared that a child named Josiah would be born in the house of David who will tear down the high places of worship. God had told the man of God not to eat bread with anyone there and not to return home the same way he came. An old prophet lied to the man of God in order to persuade the man to return home with him. He told him, "An angel spoke to me by the word of the Lord, saying, 'Bring him back with you to your house, that he may eat bread and drink water'" (1 Kings 13:18). As a result of these false words, the man of God neglected to obey what God had told him and he went with the prophet. Later, on his return home, the man of God was killed by a lion.

The thought that spoke to me while I read this story was that the man of God allowed another man to persuade him to disobey God. We have promises that have been given to us in the Bible. God may have spoken specific words to us. We may have received dreams and plans for the future that God has given us. If we are not careful, we could allow another person to minimize what God has told us and subsequently cause us to not fulfill God's purpose for our lives. If we receive a word or a dream from God, we need to hide it in our heart and don't ever let go of it.

FOOD FOR THOUGHT: Father God, I pray that we will hold on to your God given words and dreams and we will not let anyone take them from us.

GOD WAS WITH THEM

SCRIPTURE:

Be strong and of good courage, do not fear nor be afraid of them; for the Lord your God, He is the One who goes with you. He will not leave you nor forsake you. (Deuteronomy 31:6)

The book of Genesis includes a long list of people who walked with God, beginning with Adam and Eve in the Garden of Eden. Genesis 2:19 says that God brought every beast of the field and every bird of the air to Adam so that he could name them. When I first read this I was impressed with the thought that Jehovah God asked Adam to name the animals.

We also read about Enoch who walked with God and then was no more. I can imagine Enoch talking with God one minute and the next minute he was in Heaven with God, just like stepping from one room into another.

Noah walked with God and found grace in His eyes. As a result, Noah and his family were the only ones who survived the flood.

God told Abraham that He would bless him and make him a great nation. Abraham became a very wealthy man. He is known as the "Father of Faith." We are even told how Abraham had a debate with God regarding Sodom and Gomorrah before God destroyed the two cities – this gives the impression God and Abraham were not strangers, but friends.

Many times in the scriptures it states the Lord was with Joseph, even when Joseph was in prison. The disciple, Stephen, sums this story up in Acts 7:9: "And the patriarchs, becoming envious, sold Joseph into Egypt. But God was with him and delivered him out of all his troubles, and gave him favor and wisdom in the presence of Pharaoh, king of Egypt."

God talked with Moses, who led the people out of Egypt. When Moses was on the mountain with God, his countenance changed as a result of being in the presence of God.

Later when Joshua replaced Moses, after he died, God told Joshua not to be afraid because God was with him.

We have scriptures of how God also walked with Isaac, Jacob, David, Solomon, Daniel, Elijah and Elisha, to name a few.

In the Old Testament, the Spirit of God would come upon people in times of need. In the New Testament, we have a better promise. We are told that when we accept Jesus as our Lord, the Holy Spirit comes and dwells in us. We have the Spirit of God that is with us every single minute of every day. The same Spirit that raised Jesus from the dead lives in us (see Romans 8:11).

Proverbs 12:2 tells us, "A good man obtains favor from the Lord." As children of God, we have the favor of God. He will never leave us nor forsake us (see Hebrews 13:5). We are never alone. Can you imagine that the God of creation is on our side? He loves us and He wants us to succeed. All we have to do is call on Him.

FOOD FOR THOUGHT: I pray we have ears to hear what the Holy Spirit says to us. I pray we are sensitive to the leadings of the Holy Spirit. I pray that when the world sees us, they will say, "God walked with them."

I GIVE YOU ME

SCRIPTURE:

O God, You are my God, early will I seek You; My soul thirsts for You. (Psalm 63:1)

I wake up in the morning and the first thought on my mind is my Lord, God Jehovah.

I wake up in the morning, realizing you have given me another day to breathe. The cry of my heart to you is that I don't waste this day. When I lay my head down to sleep tonight, I want to hear you say, "Well done, faithful servant."

I wake up in the morning in awe that you can use me again for another day. I pray, Lord, that I hear your voice and follow the dictates of your heart. Keep me in your path, not mine.

I wake up in the morning on my knees, expecting it to be a great day. Father, I ask that I might be the avenue of great blessings to someone else. Give me a servant's heart.

I wake up in the morning, asking you to guide me through the day. I pray, Holy Spirit, that you quickly nudge me when I am about to do something that is not pleasing to my heavenly Father.

I wake up in the morning, praising the creator of the Heavens and the Earth. Only you can help and protect me from harm.

I wake up in the morning, giving myself to you. Through your son, Jesus, you have given me so much. Your forgiveness, your love, and your presence surround me with joy. I thank you for another day.

FOOD FOR THOUGHT: Father, I seek you early in the morning; I will not begin this day without seeking your face first. I begin the day with worship, because you alone are worthy of our praise. I ask you to guide my steps for the day. Thank you.

LOST SHEEP

Oh friend of Mine, please come and stay;
Abide, oh brother, you can lay
Your burdens down on Me this night;
Enter in, draw near to My light.

It's true, there's much I ask of you;
But in My rest you can find true
Release from all those trials and snares;
Enter in, you'll find who cares.

I am The Way who opens wide
To sinners who would throw aside
The world and all that it adores;
Enter in through Life's front door.

I am the Shepherd who can lead
You to green pastures which do feed
The many others won before;
Enter in, I've room for more.

When you became My sheep I prayed
Then to my Father you would lay
Your burdens down on Me this night;
Enter in, accept My light!

By Ron Massman

LOST LOVED ONES

SCRIPTURE:

Hearing you will hear and shall not understand, and seeing you will see and not perceive; for the hearts of this people have grown dull, their ears are hard of hearing and their eyes they have closed, lest they should see with their eyes and hear with their ears, lest they should understand with their hearts and turn, so that I should heal them. (Isaiah 6:9, 10; Matthew 13:14, 15)

When I get to Heaven I want to be able to see my loved ones, my parents, my spouse, my children and my friends. But there are some who have not yet chosen to believe in the provision of salvation. They have blinders on their eyes and they are unable to accept God's mercy and forgiveness. Some believe they have plenty of time to make the decision, so they are living in the world now, not realizing today may be the last day they take a breath. Some have their focus on material possessions, so they don't have time for God. While others believe they have committed the unforgivable sin and the blood of Jesus is not able to wash away their sin. Some have taken the Word of God and emphatically declared that it is not for today.

Father, it is my privilege to stand in the gap for my lost loved ones. You alone, who are omnipotent and omniscient, know what is needed to change a person's heart and draw them closer to you. Reveal to them your incredible love and help them to understand that no sin is too large for you to forgive. We know it is your will that no man should perish. Whether it takes a day or years, no matter what I see with my natural eyes, I will not let go of my hope in you to save my loved ones.

FOOD FOR THOUGHT: Father, we come before the throne of grace and ask the scales be removed from our loved ones eyes so they can see the truth. We stand on your Word for household salvation: "Believe on the Lord Jesus Christ, and you will be saved, you and your household" (Acts 16:31). As Joshua stated, "But as for me and my house, we will serve the Lord" (Joshua 24:15b). We thank you in advance for the work you are now doing to bring our loved ones, _____, home.

TREE PLANTED BY
THE RIVER OF LIFE

SCRIPTURE:

Blessed is the man who walks in the counsel of the ungodly, nor stands in the path of the sinners, nor sits in the seat of the scornful; but his delight is in the law of the Lord. And in His law he mediates day and night. He shall be like a tree planted by the rivers of water, that brings forth its fruit in its season, whose leaf shall not whither; and whatever he does shall prosper. (Psalm 1:1-3)

Psalm 1 is one of my favorite Psalms, along with Psalm 34. One day when I was praying for my children, God led me to Psalm 1. As I was reading, God gave this Psalm to me as follows...

And Joseph shall be like a tree planted (*roots are planted deep in good soil*) by the rivers of water (*whoever drinks of the water that I shall give him will never thirst* – John 4:14), Joseph shall bring forth (*much*) fruit (*I am the vine, you are the branches. He who abides in Me, and I in him, bears much fruit; for without me you can do nothing* – John 15:5) in due season; Joseph's leaf shall not writher (*If anyone does not abide in Me, he is cast out as a branch and is withered* – John 15:6) and whatsoever Joseph does shall prosper. Joseph shall not walk in the counsel of the ungodly, but Joseph shall delight in the law of the Lord.

Hallelujah. Our children, yours and mine, have the same promise. Try reading this again and put your child's name in Joseph's place.

FOOD FOR THOUGHT: God wants us to speak words of life over our lost loved ones. As God says in Isaiah 55:11, "So shall My word be that goes forth from My mouth; it shall not return to Me void, but it shall accomplish what I please, and it shall prosper in the thing for which I sent it."

FATHER GOD, A CHILD'S PRAYER

SCRIPTURE:

But Jesus said, "Let the little children come to Me, and do not forbid them; for of such is the kingdom of heaven." (Matthew 19:14)

God, this is Bobby. But you already know that. They say you like little children and you let them sit on your lap. Can I crawl up in your lap and talk to you?

Mommy and Daddy told me the boogeyman would get me if I was not asleep before dark. Father God, thank you for holding my hand until I am able to go to sleep.

My little brother is in the hospital. He is very sick. In Sunday school, I heard the teacher say that Jesus healed the sick. Father God, please heal my little brother.

Here I am again. Christmas is right around the corner. I would like a new bike for Christmas. Can you get one for my brother also? My little sister is too young for a bike. But she likes teddy bears. That is all I want this time. Thank you.

God there is a bully at school. He says mean things to me. I remember that you are with me and that I am not supposed to be afraid. But Father God, can you help the bully to know you so he won't be so mean.

Father God, Mommy and Daddy are fighting again. Their voices are loud with angry words. Please help them to stop before it is too late.

Daddy lost his job. Mommy is crying. There is no food in the house. My brother and sister and I are hungry. Father God, help Daddy find another job. I know that all things are possible with you.

Mommy and Daddy said that we are moving to another state. Daddy has found a good job there. I am a little scared. Well, to tell you the truth, I am scared a lot. I have to leave my friends and go to a strange, new school. I hope I will like the new school. Help me find a new friend.

Father God, I don't want to bother you with little things. But I really need your help this time. I have a Math test Friday. I'm not so good in Math. Please help me to understand the questions and to remember what I am supposed to do.

Father God, thank you for helping me with my SAT test. It is time for me to go to college. I know I am too big to climb on your lap, but can I sit with you a little while? I need you to help me make the right decision concerning which college I should attend. Your Word says that all wisdom comes from you. I'll wait for your answer.

Father God, as you know, I have met this beautiful woman who loves you very much. She has agreed to marry me. I am asking you to help me be a good husband.

Father God, I have an urgent prayer for you. My wife has been diagnosed with cancer. You have proven to me many times that you are our provider and healer. I thank you in advance for healing my wife.

Today I just want to thank you and praise you for your goodness. Thank you for healing my wife. Also, we want to thank you for the exciting news we received today. We are going to be parents. We will seek your face and ask your help in raising the child you are blessing us with.

Father God, I am coming to you as a father myself. My little boy will be coming to you for prayer. I know you will let him climb up in your lap and let him talk to you, just as you have let me. No matter how small or big the prayers, I know you will listen with attentive ears and you will answer his prayers. Thank you for taking good care of my son.

FOOD FOR THOUGHT: We come to you, Father God, as a little child comes to his earthly father, with that bubbling excitement, knowing we have your full attention. Just as you anticipate spending times with us, we also long to be in your presence. We don't have to speak superficial, intellectual, religious prayers. You hear the simple prayers of your children.

LIFT HIM UP

A costly price my Saviour paid.
A price not free;
His love, so true, replaced my sins,
He lifted me!

The nail scarred hands, a crown of thorns
On Calvary's tree;
A spectacle for men to see,
He lifted me!

So long ago, He shed for me
His precious blood;
How can I not but live for Him;
This one I love?

Lift Him up! Ye servants true,
The time is now!
Lift Him up! For all to see
His pierced brow!

Lift Him up! Ye must not shun
Thy Master's call!
The fruit is ripe, the time is right
To give thine all!

By Ron Massman

THE LOCKED BOX

SCRIPTURES:

I am He who lives, and was dead, and behold, I am alive forevermore. Amen. And I have the keys of Hades and of Death. (Revelation 1:18)

He who has the key of David, He who opens and no one shuts, and shuts and no one opens… (Isaiah 22:22, Revelation 3:7b)

There is a locked box that has been hidden deep down in my inner being. It has been there for a very long time. Sometimes I forget about it. Regardless of my awareness or unawareness of this locked box, it still affects my life. What is odd about this locked box is that I do not know where the key is, or even if I ever had the key. I just know there is something hidden in the box that I don't want to share with anyone in the whole wide world, not even God.

God wants me to surrender everything in my life to Him, but I am afraid to allow Him to open the locked box. I know it will hurt. But God reminds me that until I let Him open the box, He is unable to heal, restore, or replace whatever it is I have hidden in the box.

God has been so good to bring me from where I was to where I am now. He has not failed me before. I want to go deeper in the things of God. I want to know His love more. I want to be free from the pain that is hidden in that box. I pray, "God, help me to unlock the box. I don't know how and I don't have the strength to do it on my own." God hears my cry. Without my realizing it, God has maneuvered happenings in my life that has caused the box to be unlocked. My heart breaks. The tears come. "Oh God, it hurts so much."

"My child, I am here. Lean on me. Let me put my salve on the wounds."

I cry until I think I can cry no more. But I still cry. Then the moment arrives when I look into the box and I find it is now empty. The pain is gone. I am free.

FOOD FOR THOUGHT: God, I pray for the courage to come to you with everything I am, holding nothing back. I thank you in advance for helping me to face whatever it is I have locked up in the inner man.

BLIND BARTIMAEUS

SCRIPTURE:

As He went out of Jericho with His disciples and a great multitude, blind Bartimaeus, the son of Timaeus, sat by the road begging. And when he heard that it was Jesus of Nazareth, he began to cry out and say, "Jesus, Son of David, have mercy on me!" Then many warned him to be quiet; but he cried out all the more, "Son of David, have mercy on me!" So Jesus stood still and commanded him to be called. Then they called the blind man, saying to him, "Be of good cheer. Rise, He is calling you." And throwing aside his garment, he rose and came to Jesus. So Jesus answered and said to him, "What do you want Me to do for you?" The blind man said to Him, "Rabboni, that I may receive my sight." Then Jesus said to him, "Go your way, your faith has made you well." And immediately he received his sight and followed Jesus on the road. (Mark 10:46-52)

When there is a crowd surrounding us, are we embarrassed or afraid that the people might see us be demonstrative in our determined attitude to make contact with God? In the story above, the people near Bartimaeus told him to be quiet. Are we going to let anything or anyone keep us from receiving our miracle? Or are we going to be determined like Bartimaeus?

113

Just like the woman with the issue of blood, she pushed through the crowd to receive her miracle, because she knew that if she touched the hem of His garment, she would be healed. The woman was determined.

The world knows how to be determined. For example, a store advertises that they will be selling an expensive technological "hot" item for $10 to the first one hundred people. Another example is when a famous singer, actor, or preacher will be at the coliseum. People will arrive several hours before the doors open. Actually many have stayed overnight outdoors in order to beat the crowd.

Crying out loudly to God does not necessarily need to be with a loud vocal voice; but it does need to be loud spiritually. When I sing songs of praise, I sing with every fiber in my body. When I need a miracle, I remain at the altar of prayer until I receive a response. God notices a person who has a determined heart. Jesus heard Bartimaeus. As a result Bartimaeus received his miracle.

"JESUS. JESUS. JESUS."

FOOD FOR THOUGHT: Father, I know what it is like to push through the crowds and run to your altar. I pray that we will have a determined heart like Bartimaeus.

THE ROOM

SCRIPTURES:

Yea, though I walk through the valley of the shadow of death, I will fear no evil; for You are with me. (Psalm 23:4)

Do not be afraid. I am the First and the Last. I am the Living One; I was dead, and behold I am alive forever and ever. And I hold the keys of death and Hades. (Revelation 1:18 NIV)

I dreamed once about a room on the top floor of the house. The fear I encountered when approaching this room was insurmountable. My knees would shake, my heart would beat ever so quickly as if it was going to pop out of my chest, my stomach was queasy, and my head would spin. Sometimes when I thought about entering this room, I would be tormented with nightmares. As the result of this tremendous fear, I chose to avoid this room at all cost. I didn't want to face what was inside the room.

One day Jesus told me that He would go into the room with me. He was standing at the foot of the stairway, with his hands held out towards me, requesting me to come forward. I looked at the room at the top of the stairs, and I looked at Jesus. I looked back at the room. I felt a clenched hand holding my heart tightly; it was pounding so hard. Again I looked at Jesus. With my eyes focused on Him and nothing else, I took a step forward. With each step, I only looked at Jesus. When I reached Him, I saw His eyes look toward the room. As He took my hand, I inadvertently pulled back. Jesus turned to look at me and said, "You are not alone. I am with you." We very slowly climbed the stairs to the room. Before I realized it, we were standing in front of the door that led to that ROOM.

I fell at the feet of Jesus; I felt so unworthy. Jesus told me to stand, but I couldn't. I didn't want to. I always thought that I should be kneeling at the feet of Jesus. Who was I to be standing face to face with Him? It was unthinkable. But Jesus took my hand and drew me to a standing position. When my eyes met His eyes, my heart skipped a beat. Nothing in this lifetime will ever compare to the love and compassion I saw in His eyes. That one look washed away all the fears and concerns I had regarding the room. Even though the room had been locked, Jesus opened the door without the key. Of course: JESUS is the KEY. The darkness in the room was dispelled by the light of Jesus.

I became free that day. I will always remember those eyes of love and compassion. With the help of Jesus, I try not to let anything keep me from facing the *dark rooms* in my life.

FOOD FOR THOUGHT: What are you afraid to face? What is inside the *room* that is causing you not to enter? Ask Jesus to go into the room with you.

JOY

SCRIPTURE:

Do not sorrow, for the joy of the Lord is your strength. (Nehemiah 8:10)

How deep is your joy? Is it shallow like a brook drying up? Or, is it deep like a bottomless well? The joy the world offers is temporary and shallow like a dried up brook; but the joy God gives is like a deep, rushing river that never runs dry.

Joy is more than physical happiness; it is also a spiritual weapon. If we hook up with the source of this authentic joy, Jesus, we have the strength to overcome anything that crosses our path.

Medically speaking, joy and laughter is medicine for the soul. Stress, the counterpart of joy, can bring harm to our physical bodies. We are intricately and wonderfully created by God.

However, we have the responsibility to keep our bodies running like a fine-tuned, oiled, working machine.

Just like any medicine, we have a choice to dwell on the stress and problems of life or to turn to joy and laughter. When sorrow or pain tries to invade our lives, we can physically tell it to leave by focusing on God and His healing Word. Our minds cannot focus on two opposing thoughts at the same time. One of them has to depart. Let's choose joy.

Satan would like us to believe that being a Christian is dull and boring. The truth is that we have God, the creator of the universe as our Father, Jesus who freed us from the bondage of sins, and the Holy Spirit who dwells in us and guides us through each day. Being a child of God is the highest of all highs – nothing compares to it.

Joy unspeakable and full of Glory,
Flowing like a river, never to run dry.
The source of this joy is God.

FOOD FOR THOUGHT: Father, when we are hurting, we come to you, asking you to change our sorrow to joy. We let your joy wash away all the hurt. As our perfect Father, we lean on you, knowing that you alone can take care of us.

FORGIVENESS

SCRIPTURE:

No servant can serve two masters; for either he will hate the one and love the other, or else he will be loyal to the one and despise the other. You cannot serve God and mammon [riches, or anything which you trust and on which you rely]. (Luke 16:13)

And whenever you stand praying, if you have anything against anyone, forgive him and let it drop (leave it, let it go), in order that your Father Who is in heaven may also forgive you your [own] failings and shortcomings and let them drop. (Mark 11:25 The Amplified Bible)

The betrayal stings. The love of my heart left me for another. My soul breaks with an unbearable pain that cannot stop. The poison of unforgiveness has entered my heart. WHY LORD?

The words he said hurt me deeply. He was angry and I was angry. He said he was sorry. TOO LATE.

He did me harm. He stole from me. He was someone I knew and trusted. He crossed the path of my secure walls. HOW COULD THIS HAPPEN?

He molested, raped and abused me. I tried to fight him off, but I was not strong enough. I WILL NEVER FORGIVE HIM. CAN I EVER TRUST MEN AGAIN? CAN I TRUST GOD?

I was so angry at everyone. I decided to live for myself and no one else. I didn't care what they thought. So I lived a lifestyle that brought me shame. I CAN NEVER FORGIVE MYSELF.

There are many reasons we hold unforgiveness in our heart. As the scripture states, we cannot serve two masters. While we refuse to forgive, the love of God cannot flow freely as it should. The fruits of unforgiveness are destructive to our own bodies, regardless of the other person.

How can we forgive others when wrong has been done to us? Go to the cross to find the answer. Jesus was betrayed, hated, envied, lied about, scorned, abused and beaten. He had done no wrong. But that did not stop Jesus from fulfilling His destiny. He went to the cross anyway. Why? Love is the answer. He loves us so much. He paid the price so that we could be free. On the cross, Jesus said, "Father, forgive them for they do not know what they do" (Luke 23:34). Jesus shows us the way.

FOOD FOR THOUGHT: Love and unforgiveness don't mix. As we choose to forgive, God helps us to release the unforgiveness and He brings us peace. My prayer is that we choose to forgive and let God help us to walk it out.

WORSHIP

SCRIPTURE:

But the hour is coming, and now is, when the true worshipers will worship the Father in spirit and truth; for the Father is seeking such to worship Him. (John 4:23)

Jesus, as I think about you, I envision you standing before me. I am overwhelmed with the stillness of your glorious presence. Time seems to stand still as if presenting a hush for the King of Kings. I fall at your feet like a rag doll, feeling unworthy to look upon your holy face. As you reach down with your nail-scarred hands to pull me up, I hear you gently say, "My child, I love you." As I stand face to face with my Lord and Savior, I am unable to look away. Your eyes are filled with such love and compassion. The walls around my bruised heart melt away like a rushing river in a rainstorm. My arms are lifted high in surrender to the One who has redeemed me from my past. As you reach out to touch my outstretched hands, a flutter goes through my heart and my whole body, as if I were kissed by an intimate loved one. The affect of your presence leaves me speechless. I stand in awe of my Savior who gave His life for me.

Many years ago, I turned my back on you, blaming you for the pain I suffered; nevertheless, you never turned your back on me. Even when I was not following after you, you pursued me with your love. Now I stand before you, and the tears flow down my face. I don't ever want to leave your presence. I am so in love with you.

FOOD FOR THOUGHT: Jesus, I desire to worship you with my entire being. There is nothing on this Earth that compares to being in your presence. I pray that we will be a people who worship our Father in Heaven with every fiber in our body.

I AM RISEN

Oh Father, please forgive them now,
They know not what to do;
They're blind to what is Truth and Life,
Deceived by Satan's rule.

My own, your sons, are scattered now,
Confused and sore afraid;
Protect them with your mighty hand,
Until from death I'm raised.

These nails of pain I gladly bear,
God's will unveiled through Me;
This suffering, Our Love for all,
My step to make men free.

My cup is set to overflow,
The devil's fate revealed
Agape Love runs crimson red
All mankind for to heal!

I see My faithful saved at last,
Both old and new set free!
Death's sting is gone,
My body raised from grave to victory!

I am the One who conquered death,
The Lamb of God am I;
I rose to give you endless life,
As to yourself you die.

I live to see you through each day;
The joy's in Me you see;
I am the Way, the Truth and Life
You find at Calvary!

By Ron Massman

HOLY SPIRIT

SCRIPTURES:

Or do you know that your body is the temple of the Holy Spirit who is in you, whom you have from God, and you are not your own? (1 Corinthians 6:19)

But if the Spirit of Him who raised Jesus from the dead dwells in you, He who raised Christ from the dead will also give life to your mortal bodies through His Spirit who dwells in you. (Romans 8:11)

The same Spirit that lived in Jesus while he walked on Earth is the same Spirit that lives in us. The same Spirit that anointed Jesus to accomplish the things He did is the very same Spirit that anoints us to do the things that God has asked us to do.

Jesus, the Son of God, came down to Earth as a child. In Matthew 3:13-17, it explains that after John the Baptist baptized Jesus, the Spirit of God came upon Jesus. First of all Jesus was baptized by John to fulfill righteousness and then Jesus received the Holy Spirit. After this, Jesus began to fulfill his ministry and purpose with the anointing power of the Holy Spirit.

Consider this: we have the very same power that Jesus had. By receiving the Holy Spirit in our lives, we have the power to testify of the Good News to a lost and dying world. In addition, we are equipped to fight the wiles of the devil. We can draw on the anointing of the Holy Spirit to receive wisdom and knowledge beyond our own ability. According to Galatians 5:22 the fruits of the Holy Spirit are love, joy, peace, longsuffering, kindness, goodness, faithfulness, gentleness, self-control. I would not want to live this life on Earth without the help of the Holy Spirit.

The Holy Spirit can help in the little events of our daily lives. For example, I remember when I took courses for my job in order to better my status. Some of the topics were Economics, Medicine, Marketing, Actuary, and Insurance Law. There was no teacher. We would be required to read the book and then take the exam. When there was a question I did not have a clue what the answer was, I would ask the Holy Spirit to help me understand the question. After rereading the question I would be able to answer it, all because of the help of the Holy Spirit.

Many years ago I was asked by my Pastor to speak on the topic of joy. The thought of speaking before a group of people was not my cup of tea. Usually the butterflies in my stomach would cause my brain to forget what I was going to say. I asked the Holy Spirit to help me. I spoke with confidence. I felt I could have climbed the highest mountain, all because of the help of the Holy Spirit.

When my husband passed away, the Holy Spirit filled me with the grace and power of God to not succumb to the grief of the lost of my husband and best friend.

When I had major decisions to make, I would ask the Holy Spirit to help me know what God wanted me to do. He always showed me the way.

We are the temple of the Holy Spirit; therefore, the spirit of God lives in us continually. He will never leave us. We have the anointing of the Holy Spirit available 24/7. All we have to do is ask for His help.

FOOD FOR THOUGHT: Just as the song goes, we say, "Holy Spirit, you are welcome in this place."

OUR PACKAGE

SCRIPTURE:

For You formed my inward parts; You covered me in my mother's womb. I will praise You, for I am fearfully and wonderfully made; marvelous are your works, and that my soul knows very well. (Psalm 139:13)

Our life represents a package that is a culmination of all the things that makes us who we are: tall or short, plump or slim, poor or rich, educated or uneducated, gifted or challenged, young or old. What country were we born in – America, Europe, Africa, Israel…? Was our skin brown, white, red, or yellow? Were we a victim of abuse? Or was life good to us? Did we look to God or did we run from Him? Were we a child of God?

Imagine two packages on a table. One of the packages is wrapped in shiny red/gold paper with a gold colored bow on top. The other package is a brown paper bag. Which package is more appealing to the eye gate? Which package would a person select?

Some packages are beautifully wrapped, but empty inside; while other packages are ruffled and dingy on the outside, but filled with gold and precious jewels. Some packages stand out above others. These usually receive more attention, while others are neglected.

We tend to want the beautifully wrapped packages that shine. We may even resent our own package, especially when we compare our package with others. We may wish, "Only if I was packaged like them."

But God knew us from the beginning, even as we were formed in our mother's womb. He has a specific plan for our lives that only we can fulfill. We need to embrace our package and live our life for the glory of God.

FOOD FOR THOUGHT: Father, I thank you that we are awesomely created by the hand of God. I pray that we will not compare ourselves with others, because we are all individually made; there are no duplicates. Let us be content with "our package" and strive to fulfill the destiny you have planned for us.

RUNNING THE RACE

SCRIPTURE:

Therefore, we also, since we are surrounded by so great a cloud of witnesses, let us lay aside every weight, and the sin which so easily ensnares us, and let us run with endurance the race that is set before us, looking unto Jesus, the author and finisher of our faith...(Hebrews 12:1, 2)

Blinders are placed on horses to restrict their vision to the rear and side. This method is used to keep them from being distracted, helping the horses focus on what is in front of them.

We have a race to run. The finish line is ahead – the day we go home to Heaven and are able to see Jesus face to face. Do we cross the finish line, knowing there were things God wanted us to do, but we didn't do them? Do we let the flesh keep us from knowing what it is like to walk in victory? Or, do we make it to the end, knowing that we have followed after God with our whole heart, mind, soul and body.

In this race, there are many distractions. At any moment in a day, we can be distracted by thoughts from the devil. Our minds are constantly bombarded with negative thoughts. We are distracted by things that pull us from the love of God. We even become distracted by daily living and doing good things. All these distractions make it difficult to hear the quiet voice of the Holy Spirit talking to us.

My desire is to stay focused on God, by reading His Word, talking to Him, and listening to the Holy Spirit. I put on spiritual blinders so I am not distracted while I am running this race, called life.

FOOD FOR THOUGHT: Father, with the help of the Holy Spirit, we put on spiritual blinders so we are not distracted by the things of this world. We determine to keep our focus on you.

THE MIND OF CHRIST

SCRIPTURE:

But we have the mind of Christ. (1 Corinthians 2:16)

In Romans 12:2 God tells us through the words of Paul, "Do not be conformed to this world, but be transformed by the renewing of your mind that you may prove what is that good and acceptable and perfect will of God." Our minds are being bombarded every minute by thoughts, some good and some bad. In order for our minds to be conformed to the mind of Christ, we must be very careful what we think about. In Philippians 4:8, Paul explains, "Finally, brethren, whatever things are *true*, whatever things are *noble,* whatever things are *just*, whatever things are *pure*, whatever things are *lovely*, whatever things are of *good report*, if there is any *virtue* and if there is anything *praiseworthy* – meditate on these things."

We have a choice. Do we let our minds think about what is true, noble, just, pure, lovely, of good report, virtuous, and praiseworthy? Or, do we let our minds be filled with lustful thoughts, gossip, discouraging or negative words, bad reports, or things that are not acceptable to God. If God could hear what we are thinking, which He can, would we be embarrassed.

In 1 Thessalonians 5:22, Paul tells us to "abstain from every form of evil." This includes physical action AND thoughts of the mind. In order for our minds to be renewed and transformed, we need to read the Word of God. According to Hebrews 4:12, "the Word of God is living and powerful, and sharper than any two-edged sword, piercing even to the division of soul and spirit, and of joints and marrow, and is a discerner of the thoughts and intents of the heart."

Joyce Meyers has written a book on this subject called *Battlefield of the Mind.* It is a battle. Satan wants to bombard our thoughts with wrong thinking so that our minds are not renewed towards living the way God wants us to. God wants to fill our minds with His thoughts and His plans. Philippians 4:7 states "The peace of God, which surpasses all understanding, will guard your hearts and minds through Christ Jesus." We can have a mind of peace, not a mind of torment. It all depends on what we allow to make home in our mind. The choice is ours.

FOOD FOR THOUGHT: Father it is so easy to accept the thoughts of our mind as normal if we do not know what the Bible says. When the devil tries to instill a wrong mode of thinking, we need to dissipate it with the Word of God. We need to meditate on the Word so we are filled with the power and strength to stand against the wiles of the devil.

REBUILDING THE HIGH PLACES

SCRIPTURE:

He rebuilt the high places his father Hezekiah had destroyed; he also erected altars to Baal and made an Asherah pole, as Ahab king of Israel had done. He bowed down to all the starry hosts and worshiped them. (2 Kings 21:3 NIV)

We have asked God to tear down strongholds in our lives that keep us bound. They could include anything from smoking, drugs, alcohol, and overeating to pornography, gambling or fowl language. We attend conferences where we write down the strongholds on a sheet of paper, tell God that we are sorry, repent and turn from the sins or addictions that have ensnared us. We go home feeling free and victorious with our clean slate of starting over afresh. We may do fine for a period of time. Then one day an event in our lives may trigger the pull to open the door again to the stronghold we had turned from. For example, we may decide to quit smoking. A stressful situation crosses our path. The desire for a cigarette becomes stronger and stronger as we imagine the smell or taste of the cigarette. As we entertain the thought, we imagine what it would be like to have the cigarette and exhale the stress of the situation. Then before we know it, we have smoked a cigarette. We have opened the door for the stronghold to take over again.

When I read the phrase, "He rebuilt the high places," it resonated in my spirit. The Bible states King Hezekiah had removed the high places of worship to false gods. He did what was right in the sight of God. However, Manasseh rebuilt the high places which Hezekiah, his father, had destroyed. He did what was evil in the sight of God. Then it became clear in my spirit that we must be careful not to build up the high places in our lives, not to allow the doors to be reopened to those strongholds that God has delivered us from. If we have been freed from the bondage of alcohol, we don't want to enter a bar. If we have been freed from pornography, then we do not allow our eye gates to entertain such pictures. Whatever we have been freed from, we don't allow our mind to entertain those thoughts. The minute a wrong thought tries to invade our mind; we must turn from it completely and think about something that is good. Philippians 2:12-13 implores us to work out our salvation in fear and trembling.

FOOD FOR THOUGHT: Matthew 12:43-45 conveys a story about a man who had cleaned his house of an evil spirit. When this evil spirit was unable to find a resting place, he returns to the man's house, finding it unoccupied and swept clean. Then he locates seven evil spirits worse than himself and they return to the house to abide in it. "The final condition of that man is worse than the first" (Matthew 12:45 NIV). When we are delivered from strongholds, we must fill the clean house with righteous things of God.

JOB

Undeserved, which was my plea,
Your fiery judgment set on me!
Your wrath, oh God, became my ear;
Until your Grace itself was reared.

From dark despair to peace of mind,
Such joy you give despite those times
I was the master of my soul;
Until your Grace to me you showed.

I know that my Redeemer lives!
I thank you Lord for thoughts that give
Me insight to your holy plan;
That by your Grace I now can stand.

I now live by your pledge alone,
Oh sovereign God, You will atone
For all my sins both great and small;
As Grace one day will give its all.

When I've been there 10,000 years,
I'll sing your praise through many tears
Of joy I shed that glorious day,
When by your Grace my soul you saved.

By Ron Massman

BAD THINGS HAPPEN

SCRIPTURES:

Trust in the Lord with all your heart, and lean not on your own understanding; in all thy ways acknowledge Him, and He shall direct your paths. (Proverbs 3:5, 6)

"For My thoughts are not your thoughts, nor are your ways My ways," says the Lord. (Isaiah 55:8)

When God says "No", do I have the right attitude, believing God has my best interest; or, do I get angry? When it appears God has turned his back on me, do I turn my back on Him?

Who am I to argue with God? How dare I have the audacity to get mad at God? The truth is that I did get mad at God when something bad happened to my children; however, God's love, mercy, and understanding for a devastated soul were greater than my yelling at God in anger. The creator of the universe did not strike me down dead (a theological thought that had been rendered to me in my upbringing). I don't say this frivolously. He knew my heart.

Tragic events such as suicide, rape, death, murder, abuse, loss of home and possessions may seem more than we can handle. The pain is unbearable. We ask God why He allowed these devastating events to happen. We wonder why He didn't step in and stop them from happening? He could have. Why? Why? Why?

We may never know the answer until we see God face to face. We live in a fallen world, where man has free choice.

Why did God allow His son, Jesus to die such a horrible death on the cross? He could have sent a legion of angels to stop it. We know that because God loved us, He said "No" to Jesus, and allowed Jesus to die on that rugged cross – for us.

We know that because of the cross, we have an advocate with God. If something happens, He can take the broken pieces and put them back together again. Whatever God allows in our lives can be used to draw us closer to Him, remove impurities from our lives, and change us to be more like Him. For that we give God the glory.

FOOD FOR THOUGHT: Father, I understand the pain of being raped, losing my best friend in a car accident, watching my husband die from an illness even though I believed for his healing, losing my home and all my possessions, and much more. Some of these tragic events brought anger; while some brought a knowing trust. I ask you to forgive us when we get angry. Hold us up as you do in that popular poem, "Footprints."

SUFFERING FOR JESUS

SCRIPTURE:

For to you it has been granted on behalf of Christ, not only to believe in Him, but also to suffer for His sake. (Philippians 1:29)

A soldier usually fights with pride for his country and if that same soldier is injured, or even killed, he is considered a hero. If a Christian is a missionary in a foreign country and he suffers loss for Jesus, when he gets to heaven he is awarded a "crown of life" for the suffering (see Revelation 2:10).

In cases of war we can accept suffering because we know there is a reason for it. But there are times when it is not so obvious and straightforward that we have suffered for a just cause. There are things that happen in our lives where we do not see the good purpose for it. For example, when a parent loses a child or a good person is shot, we sometimes wonder what is right and good about that.

Suffering entails our attitude in the process of suffering. Do we deal with suffering in a righteous way, or do we let the incident infect us with bitterness or anger? Do we let sin rise up in us because we are unable to accept something that has occurred to us which we think is not right? It may be easier to suffer for a just cause, but when the cause is a tragic occurrence, how do we handle it?

Do we handle our suffering with grace or do we say, "How could this possibly happen to me?" Do we ask God to help us get through this season of grieving and suffering, or do we park our lives in that spot of grieving and not go forward?

Romans 8:28 tells us that everything works out to good for those who love God. I agree that this is a very hard phrase to accept when you are hurting. When people spoke this to me, I would get offended.

Consider this – Jesus suffered on the cross, but He did not lash out at those who caused the suffering. He asked God to forgive them. Jesus exemplifies the ultimate attitude we should strive for when we suffer.

FOOD FOR THOUGHT: God, you know what it was like to watch your own son, Jesus, suffer on the cross; however, you did not let this stop you from loving the people who caused the hurt. We can learn to handle our suffering the same way you did. We need your grace to help us do this.

HEM OF HIS GARMENT

SCRIPTURES:

And suddenly, a woman who had a flow of blood for twelve years came from behind and touched the hem of His garment. For she said to herself, "If only I may touch His garment, I shall be made well." (Matthew 9:20, 21)

But Jesus said, "Somebody touched Me, for I perceived power [virtue] going out from Me." (Luke 8:46)

When my husband died as the result of an illness, I determined in my heart to worship God at the altar. In tears I cried, "If only I could touch the hem of your garment, my heart would stop aching with grief."

When sickness and pain caused me to function with limitations, I prostrated myself at the altar and pleaded with God, "If only I could touch the hem of your garment, I know I would be healed."

When my son decided to disinherit his family, I bowed down at the altar and cried out, "If only I could touch the hem of your garment, I know God can heal my broken heart and restore my son."

When my second husband betrayed me and divorce was the conclusion, I fell on my knees before God and cried, "If only I could touch the hem of your garment, I know you can give my life purpose again."

When I had to give up my home, my job, and move away from my friends, I reached out and touched the hem of His garment. I knew He would pull me out of the deep well of despair and provide a future for me.

When depression surrounded me like a cloak of darkness, I crawled to the altar and I cried out, "If only I could touch the hem of your garment, I know my soul could be restored and that you would give me hope again."

Each time I knew that if I could touch the hem of His garment and not let go, Jesus would provide the answer. Each moment when His virtue or power was released in my life, it was like a hug from God. Nothing in this life compares.

FOOD FOR THOUGHT: Father, like the woman with the issue of blood who touched the hem of Jesus' garment, we likewise grab on and refuse to let go until we receive that hug from you.

WINGS

Some men have paper wings designed
By them to sail the skies;
Thus weighted down and burned out long
Before they start to rise.

Soaring far above the fray,
Intent oh lofty realms;
Eagle wings of just resolve,
Too high to be put down.

Those seeds of hope on gamut wings,
To and fro they glide;
The storms of life...Too much a task;
Much less be true or tried!

Remember friend, My burden's light,
Come trust and follow Me;
I'll give you wings of spirit cast,
As in the fray you'll be.

Though to and fro in earthly haunts,
Each day with strife anew;
Have courage, friend, I've overcome
The world and so will you!

By Ron Massman

SOARING LIKE AN EAGLE

SCRIPTURES:

But those who wait on the Lord shall renew their strength; they shall mount up with wings like eagles, they shall run and not be weary, they shall walk and not faint. (Isaiah 40:31)

He who dwells in the secret place of the Most High, shall abide under the shadow of the Almighty. (Psalm 91:1)

Who satisfies your mouth with good things, so that your youth is renewed like the eagle's. (Psalm 103:5)

What a wonderful picture of what it is like to soar as an eagle and live under the wings of God's protection. There is no safer place to abide.

As insurmountable boulders block the pathway of life, I ascend high above the physical realm into the presence of God. When the storms of life seem more than I can handle, I imagine soaring like an eagle high above it all. With my arms raised, I am gliding with ease, knowing nothing can touch me. At that height, the problems seem miniscule and insignificant, just as people, cars, and buildings appear to be the size of ants from an airplane.

The bill of an eagle is capable of tearing the flesh from tough carrion into small, bite size pieces. In a similar way, as I speak the Word of God, it tears apart the schemes of the devil. Just as the eagle has the ability to see detail at a distance, I am filled with the wisdom of God, able to discern the ways of God and man. I am free like the eagle to soar above the Earth in the same manner as Jesus has given me freedom to live this life in victory.

The glory of God's majesty is unveiled as the eagle soars high above with long, broad wings with characteristic splayed fingertips. In likewise manner, I raise my arms high above, my heart soaring like an eagle, to give praise to the One and Only true God, who can hide me under his wings of protection.

FOOD FOR THOUGHT: Father God, I pray we will come to you immediately when the weight of our problems brings us down. As you lift us high above on eagle's wings, you shall renew our strength. We shall know your protection.

HOW HIGH DO YOU WANT TO FLY

SCRIPTURE:

Nevertheless I am continually with You; You hold me by my right hand. You will guide me with Your counsel, and afterward receive me to glory. Whom have I in Heaven but You? And there is none upon earth that I desire besides You. My flesh and my heart fail; but God is the strength of my heart and my portion forever. (Psalm 73:23-26)

These verses pulled me through some dark and tumultuous storms. "He holds me with His right hand." This puts a thrill in my heart, knowing that the creator of the universe is on my side. It humbles me to realize I would not be here today, except for the grace of God. God is the best attorney, counselor, financial advisor, doctor, discerner of right and wrong, provider... You name it and He is Number One.

The question is, "How high do we want to fly?" Do we place limits on what God can do in our lives? Do we ask Him for help, or do we try to do it all by ourselves?

I want the very best that God has for me. I want to fulfill my destiny here on Earth. I want to reach higher ground, areas that all by myself I would not be able to accomplish. I want to hear His voice and be ready to step out in faith and do whatever He has asked me to do. THIS MEANS TOTAL SURRENDER TO GOD AND HIS WAYS.

Ponder these thoughts. When we are flying high, our feet are not touching the ground. The safety net is God. Also, the higher we fly, the closer we are to God and to becoming more like Him.

FOOD FOR THOUGHT: Father, I know as we trust you with our lives, you will bring us to places of accomplishment that we would never have dreamed of. I pray we will let go of the safety net and look to you alone for our provision.

HEAVEN, OUR REAL HOME

SCRIPTURE:

In My Father's house are many mansions; if it were not so, I would have told you. I go to prepare a place for you. (John 14:2)

As Dorothy, in the Wizard of Oz, clicked her sparkling ruby red shoes, she kept saying, "I want to go home. I want to go home. I want to go home." What about us? Which home is our heart loyal to? Is it our temporary home here on Earth? Or, is it our real home in Heaven with our Father, the creator of the universe? There have been times while in the midst of intense worship with my Lord that I wanted so much to go home to be with Him forever and not return. But God reminded me I am His ambassador and I still have work to do. The day will come when I can finally go home. I anxiously await that glorious day.

We are not of this world; our home is from above. We see our eternal home as through a haze, not clearly. But there will be a day our eyes will see our final destination.

We have been told by our heavenly Father that there will be no pain, no sickness, no death, no wars, no strife, no sadness, no tears, no fear, no worry, no addictions, nor chains of bondage that enslave us. Jesus is the light, now and forever, who wipes away all the darkness and evil of this world. Our eyes have not seen and our ears have not heard the possibilities of all that God has prepared for us. Even the greatest things on this Earth do not compare with what is waiting in Heaven.

Imagine the fullness of the sound of music resonating through the air? Hear the angels singing, "Holy, Holy, Holy is the Lamb of God." No choir on Earth will match the sound. The melodies will fill our hearts with glorious praise.

Colors will be richer and brighter than we have seen before. Fragrances and aromas will have the elegance of royalty. Our taste pallets will be tantalized and satisfied with heavenly food. As we touch the flowers and plants, our fingers will feel the richness and detail. Our joy will be unspeakable and our laughter will be pure and clean. The riches of our senses will surpass our imagination.

Since there is no darkness or death or destruction in Heaven, everything will be fresh. Nothing will die. We will stand in awe of the beauty of God's creation.

We will see our loved ones again. All the suffering and pain over their loss here on Earth will completely vanish. The joy of this family reunion will be incomprehensible. We will even fellowship with the biblical forefathers – such as Adam, Noah, Abraham, Moses, David, Peter and Paul. I look forward to meeting Mary, the mother of Jesus, or Queen Esther, or Anna, the prophetess. The names are endless.

According to God's Word, He is no respecter of persons (see Acts 10:34). We are all considered equal in His eyes. We will see ourselves as God envisions us – a special people and a royal generation who will reign with Him for eternity. There will be no condemnation; we will wear white robes of righteousness.

In return, we will finally understand the fullness of God's love, mercy, grace, and compassion. The mysteries of God will no longer be hidden. Here on Earth, we partially tap into the greatness of all that God has provided for us. However, in Heaven we will no longer have a veil over our minds.

On Earth everything is bound by time. In Heaven, time will not have a hold on us. We will sit at the feet of Jesus for many hours, as if it were but a moment. We may not now comprehend the movement of time in the eternity of Heaven, but in Heaven this mystery will be clear to us.

We are not abandoned here on Earth to deal with life on our own. We can walk with the same anointing as Jesus. The kingdom of God is ours to possess now. We have a foretaste of the goodness of God.

Our minds and hearts will not be prepared for the moment when we actually enter into God's presence. Will we be able to stand or will we fall at His feet in worship?

We get excited about the birth of a child, the receiving of presents on birthdays or Christmas, going on an incredible vacation, or the excitement of a football game. We should be even more excited about Heaven. There should be an unquenchable feeling of homesickness. Our hearts should have a burning desire for the day we will see Jesus face to face. Let nothing keep us from our final destination.

Remain focused on God, just like a running horse with blinders on the sides of his eyes. Are we running to Him with the same intensity of love that He has for us?

Our Daddy is waiting for us. He has prepared a glorious home for us. Are we ready to go home?

FOOD FOR THOUGHT: Father, help us each day to remember that our real home is in Heaven with you. We long for the day that we will see you face to face; however, while we are on Earth we can still experience what it is like to have Heaven on Earth: love, joy, peace, hope, wisdom, self-control, longsuffering, goodness, kindness, strength and faithfulness. All these, and more, have been given to us by Christ Jesus. Thank you.

GOD'S HANDIWORK

SCRIPTURE:

This is the day the Lord has made; we will rejoice and be glad in it. (Psalm 118:24)

In the cool breeze of the morning, as I was sitting on the porch swing outside my log cabin, I watched the sun slowly peep across the horizon – pushing the darkness away, producing glimmering reflections on the lake. In the silence of the morning, music filled the air with birds chirping their love song to each other. If I listened closely, I could hear the forest awaken with the various animal sounds. A squirrel scampered up the pine tree that hovered above the shed next to the cabin.

I looked to the sun again, which now was higher in the sky. In these moments when I said good morning to God, I sensed such peace and strength. I watched God's creation come alive under the morning sun.

The trees that blanketed the mountains surrounding the lake slowly revealed its luminous fall colors, reminding me of God's handiwork. Winter had already begun to make its invasion on the tip of the highest mountain.

Yesterday was gone forever. Tomorrow has not come yet. Today was arising.

After placing my cup of coffee on the porch railing, I sauntered to the edge of the lake, enjoying the feel of the wet grass under my feet. When I reached the lake, I rolled up my pajama legs and waded in the shallow. The chill jolted my body and without thinking I took a step backwards. With boldness, I then ran into the water, letting it splash on my legs.

In the middle of the lake, I watched a bass make the water ripple when he dove up out and then splashed back under the water's surface. Even a fish could speak to me of God's excitement for living.

As the sun rose fully above the mountain, I was faced with beginning my new day. I thanked God for reminding me how awesome He is. I knew that I could handle whatever came across my path, because the creator of the universe was with me.

FOOD FOR THOUGHT: God, our surroundings reveal your creation. Your handiwork leaves me speechless. You created this world for us to enjoy. Let us take time each day to thank you for all that you have given us. Enjoying your creation brings pleasure to you.

AT THE CROSS

SCRIPTURE:

Out of that terrible **travail of soul**, he'll see that it's worth it and be glad he did it. Through what he experienced, my righteous one, my servant, will make many "righteous ones," as he himself carries the burden of their sins. (Isaiah 53:11 The Message Bible)

…having wiped out the handwriting of requirements that was against us, which was contrary to us. And He has taken it out of the way, having nailed it to the cross. (Colossians 2:14)

The cross is where I first saw the light…where I discerned my Lord Jesus' body and ALL that He has done for me.

Maybe I have been the only person guilty of the following thought, but whenever I considered the cross, I visualized the body (the flesh) of Jesus, the outside vessel that was crucified. I've read about the 39 stripes Jesus received, the crown of thorns, the stab wound, the hands and feet nailed to the cross. These are all physical forces that bruised the outside of my Lord's body. There is more to the cross than just the physical aspects. What about His soul, His mind? At the cross, not only was His body crucified, but every feature of Jesus – His soul, His mind, His emotions, His inner self.

In order to obtain total redemption for mankind, Jesus had to suffer both physically and emotionally. Jesus, an innocent man, paid the price. He felt the pain of our punishment. Jesus knew what it was like to be beaten, rejected, mocked, betrayed, sneered at, and alone. He witnessed the inner emotional pain; therefore, He knew what it was like to be human. He was the complete package – the outer and inner self. He was crucified on the cross so we could know complete freedom in every aspect of our being.

We were the sinners, not Jesus. We were the ones who were guilty, not Jesus. We were the ones who should have appeased the wrath of God. But we couldn't. We didn't. Jesus did.

It is unfathomable to comprehend all Jesus did for us. Because of the cross, we know we are saved from eternal damnation. But also at the cross, there is forgiveness, deliverance, peace of mind, God's love and protection, wisdom, healing (both physical and emotional), provision for a blessed life, and much more. In order to receive a gift, we must reach out to possess it. If we do not know the gift is available, we are unable to receive the gift.

FOOD FOR THOUGHT: Father, help us to discern all that Jesus has done for us at the cross. I pray that once we have revelation knowledge of what Jesus bought for us with His life, we will take possession of that gift, the complete package and not only portions of it.

THE BLOOD OF JESUS

SCRIPTURES:

In Him we have *redemption* through His blood, the forgiveness of sins, according to the riches of His grace. (Ephesians 1:7)

The blood of Jesus Christ His Son *cleanses* us from all sin. (1 John 1:7)

But God demonstrates His own love toward us, in that while we were still sinners, Christ died for us. Much more then, having now been *justified* by His blood, we shall be saved from wrath through Him. (Romans 5:8, 9)

Therefore Jesus also, that He might *sanctify* the people with His own blood, suffered outside the gate. (Hebrews 13:12)

Moses spoke to the Israelites:
The angel of death will pass over the land.
During the darkness of night,
The first born son will die at its hand.

You must take a lamb without blemish,
A male of the first year.
The slaughter of this lamb is God's wish,
Taking the place of your first born son.

Dip hyssop in the lamb's blood,
Cover the doorposts and lentil of the house.
Do not cover the threshold with the blood;
It is not to be trampled on as you leave the house.

The angel of death will see the blood
That covers the doorposts of the house.
All because of the lamb's blood,
He will pass over that house.

The Passover represents a foreshadow of the cross,
How the blood is a covering for God's people.
Because of the blood of Jesus shed at the cross,
He has paved a way between God and the people.

We have been forgiven and cleansed from our
filthiness.
Our past no longer has a hold over us.
We now wear a robe of righteousness,
Given to us by Christ Jesus.

The blood of Jesus speaks of redemption;
We have been bought back from the hands of Satan.
The blood of Jesus speaks of sanctification;
We have been set apart for God's plan.

The blood of Jesus shows us how to defeat Satan.
All we have to do is speak of the blood of Jesus.
And the enemy of destruction
Has no choice but to pass over us.

Because of the blood of Jesus' victorious win,
We are now children of God.
We have been set free from the wages of sin.
We can boldly enter into the presence of God.

FOOD FOR THOUGHT: Nothing but the blood of Jesus can satisfy the wrath of God regarding rebellion and the sin nature, build a bridge between God and man, forgive us for our sins, set us free from the wages of sin, redeem us from the clutches of Satan, and sanctify us and set us apart for God's purpose. Father, we thank Jesus for being obedient to the cross and shedding His blood so we could be redeemed from death and become children of God. I pray that the blood of Jesus will never become common place in our hearts. As we plead the blood of Jesus over our lives, we give Satan a knockout punch.

A MOMENT IN TIME

SCRIPTURES:

But seek first the kingdom of God and His righteousness, and all these things shall be added to you. (Matthew 6:33)

But those who wait on the Lord shall renew their strength; they shall mount up with wings like eagles, they shall run and not be weary, they shall walk and not faint. (Isaiah 40:31)

I heard the birds singing today,
And I thought of you.
I stood still for a moment,
To breathe in spring's aroma.
I felt the sun on my face.
The warmth reminded me of your grace.
Life tried to draw me away,
But I chose to linger and soak in your peace.
I heard the river in the distance.
The bubbling of water sounded like joyous laughter.
I felt the breeze through the trees.
I listened and heard your voice.
"I am here with you, I will never leave you."
I saw the eagle soar high above.
My arms became like wings,
Lifted high in praise of you.
As I was lost in the moment of time,

I knew this touch from you would see me through the day.

FOOD FOR THOUGHT: Abba Father, let us take time each day, even if it is only for a moment, to say thank you and to tell you that we love you.

LOVE'S WAY

In silent meditation sweet,
I marvel at my Saviour's feet,
The way He died for me that day,
His Love that drew my sins away!

In loving arms that hold me now,
A Love expressed in Truth's clear vow:
In mansions bright He'll set me free,
To live with Him eternally!

How could I then compare my love
With Christ's and His redeeming blood?
Could my attempt, so fleshly based,
Do justice to His matchless grace?

Could I forget how He once cried,
While in the garden before He died?
The bitter sweat, as drops of blood,
That cup of death before Him stood?

The prayer He gave, so vital then,
Prepared this One who knew no sin;
For grief, betrayal took their toll,
'till stress beyond all limits sowed.

As He prayed "not my will but Thine",
His Father strengthened Him in time
To drink my cup, what it possessed,
And fill it back with life and rest.

My love, though not divine and true,
Perfected His to make it new;
For Christ, as He arose that day,
Latched both His Love and mine to stay!

That love, more precious than silver or gold,
Becomes my strength in times of woe,
Sustains me when my heart is weak,
Finds me when it's Him I seek.

Teaches me what's just and fair,
Guides me onto heights so rare;
Corrects me when I miss His call;
His Love to me: My all in all!

By Ron Massman

AT THE BOTTOM OF THE PIT, JESUS WAS WAITING

SCRIPTURES:

I called on your name, O Lord, from the depths of the pit. (Lamentations 3:55 NIV) I am He who lives, and was dead, and behold, I am alive forevermore. Amen. And I have the keys of Hades and of Death. (Revelation 1:18)

Our God is the God of salvation; and to God the Lord belong escapes from death. (Psalm 68:20)

When I was a child, this world seemed like a fairy tale story of a safe place to live, where there were no fears or harm knocking on the door. Our home was like a soft, warm, cuddly blanket on a cold winter night. We may have been poor, but poverty was not felt in a home where there was food on the table each and every meal. I was blessed with a mom and a dad that remained together through thick and thin. My dad worked in a factory. My mom worked at home, taking care of the family. My world consisted of my family and school. If there was evil, its residence was far, far away.

I knew God; our family went to church every Sunday. But honestly, I didn't know Him in a personal way. My trust was in my earthly daddy.

After I left the security of my parents' home, evil came knocking on my door. I was introduced to people who could not be trusted and who lulled me away from God's truth with their worldly advice. Betrayal and desertion by loved ones left me with high walls built around my heart. People broke into our home and stole treasures and memories that could never be replaced. Invasion came even closer when a man ripped my virtue from me and shame became my bed partner. Death, both of a loved one and of unfinished dreams, came with pains that could not be comforted with a pat on the back and the phrase "all things work out to good." Scars of rejection and loneliness penetrated the door of my heart until the darkness of depression surrounded me day and night. The weight of the pain became unbearable and it dragged me down into the deep, dark pit of hell.

Then a voice in the darkness pointed me to the real truth. *At the bottom of the deep crevices where no one could find me, Jesus was waiting to lift me up and bring me to a place where the light shines.* He pushed away the darkness, fears, worries, rejections, grief, and pains of life. We cannot walk in this world without Him. He alone makes sense out of all the wrongness that touches our lives. He turns weeping to joy, poverty to plenty, and rejection to belonging to the only One who can protect and take care of us.

In my angry, hurting, destructive years, when I walked in the world, I told God where to go (hell). Later, Jesus told me He actually went there and obtained the keys of hell and death. When my life fell into a deep pit of depression that almost led me to

164

physical death, God was there all along, waiting for me, to restore me to life and to Him.

When I was young, I saw through the eyes of a child. When I grew older, life touched me. Now because of Jesus I see through His eyes of truth and love. Oddly enough, now I feel safe and secure again; the evil is on the outside. As I trust God and walk with Him in intimate fellowship, He is my refuge and my protector.

FOOD FOR THOUGHT: Remember whatever deep pit that you find yourself in, Jesus is there waiting to lift you out. Call on Him. He is the answer.

THE LIGHT AT THE END
OF THE TUNNEL

SCRIPTURE:

I have come as a light into the world, that whoever believes in Me should not abide in darkness. (John 12:46)

The darkness is invading my surroundings, slowly, like a fog. At first, I did not notice the fog, but now it's suffocating me. Before I realized what was happening, I was encompassed in darkness. It's all I can see.

What has happened to my joy? Where is the peace I used to have? Then the voices come. They keep gnawing at my mind. The eerie voices are gleefully declaring, "There is no hope. There is no future. We have you now."

I hold my head in my hands as my body draws up into a fetal position. The weight of the darkness is stifling me. The pain of those voices is deafening. Why won't they be quiet? I want the pain to stop and the voices to go away. But I can't move. The voices have taken away my will to fight. I have no desire to get up. For me, there is no tomorrow. More and more, the darkness becomes my presence.

"Oh God!" I cry out. "Where are you?"

Far, far away in the distance, I see a pinhole of light. As I focus on the light, it grows bigger. At that moment, I turn my back on the darkness and I turn to the light. Eventually my eyes are able to see the source. Jesus. My heart cries out, "Jesus, I need you. I am drowning in this darkness." The light becomes brighter and brighter, closer and closer. The darkness is dissipating. "Yes. Yes. Jesus come. I remember now. You are my joy. You are my peace. Yes. Come closer." The light pushes the darkness away. The dark, grinding, evil voices leave. Now, as I focus on the light, all I hear is the voice of God.

God gently tells me, "I love you. I am here. You are not alone. I will help you. Take my hand."

God's love fills my heart with peace and joy. I take the hand of Jesus. I feel safe. I now have hope. There is a tomorrow and I know I can go on. The darkness is gone. The light prevails.

FOOD FOR THOUGHT: The feelings of darkness can surround a person who feels they are at the end of their rope. It could be when walking through financial devastation, grieving over the loss of a loved one, dealing with a terminal illness or a tragedy, or fighting off depression.

Sometimes, this darkness can lure a person into thoughts of suicide. Depression can be a blanket that hides the light. But when we look to Jesus, who is the author of light, the darkness can be dispelled by the light. Father God, I bind that spirit of depression off your children. In the name of Jesus, I ask that you will snatch them away from the pull of the evil

one who is trying to drag them down into the darkness. Let your light shine into their hearts. Let your
love restore them to wholeness of mind. Bring into
their paths whosoever is your avenue of restoration.
Thank you.

GIVE IT TO ME

SCRIPTURES:

For His anger is but for a moment, His favor is for life; weeping may endure for a night, but joy comes in the morning. (Psalm 30:5)

...but your sorrow will be turned into joy. (John 16:20)

God has an incredible exchange program: life for death, joy for sorrow, health for sickness, peace for torment, wealth for poverty, righteousness for shame.....

When I was in college, events happened that caused incredible pain. As a result of the mistakes I made, shame took hold of my life. I felt I had disappointed my parents; I did not fulfill their expectations. I covered up the shame and disappointment for forty plus years in many different ways: being shy or playing the clown, attempts at suicide, drinking, smoking, and overeating. Recently in an effort to return to the past and deal with the shame, the pain of remembrance caused me to cry uncontrollably. I thought my heart was going to break, so I cried out to God, "The pain hurts."

In the midst of the tears that was washing my face I heard, "Give it to me."

The words were so clear they interrupted my crying, and I said, "Huh?"

Again I heard, "Give it to me." By this time, God had my attention. With my spiritual eyes, I saw His arms reaching toward me with His palms up and He said, "Give me the shame."

In compliance to His request, the shame I had been holding inside me all these years was handed over to a loving God who wanted to heal my broken heart. Amazingly joy replaced the tears. I know I had an encounter with God at that moment and I experienced God's incredible exchange program.

FOOD FOR THOUGHT: Father God, help us to give to you the hurts, the mistakes, the pain, the fears, the sorrows, or anything that has been a hindrance or a stronghold in our lives.

GOD HAS A GOOD PLAN FOR US

SCRIPTURE:

For I know the thoughts that I think toward you, says the lord, thoughts of peace and not of evil, to give you a future and a hope. (Jeremiah 29:11)

When tragedy came into my life, the initial thoughts that invaded my mind were that I had no future. A friend gave me verse Jeremiah 29:11. When I became depressed, I would repeat this verse. I even have a plaque by my bed with this scripture on it. God has been faithful to bring me through the sadness and grief of the death of my husband. He has given me hope and a future. This is my testimony.

I have heard of others that have faced a tragedy in their lives. When they arrived on the other side of the pain and grief, they have also testified that God has used them to help others who are going through the same thing.

Tragedies can hit our lives hard, especially if they come unexpectedly. Sometimes the pain seems unbearable. Some people, including me, use food, alcohol or drugs to cover up the pain. But only God can bring us through this season of tragedy, without adverse effects. As long as we breathe and are here on Earth, God has a plan for us. With God in the middle of the plan, He gives us a purpose for living.

FOOD FOR THOUGHT: Father, for those who are facing a tragedy, I ask that you remind them of Jeremiah 29:11. As they seek you, you will guide and help them. Thank you.

GOD'S TIMING

SCRIPTURE:

But as for me, my prayer is to You, O Lord, in the acceptable time; O God in the multitude of Your mercy, hear me in the truth of Your salvation. (Psalm 69:13)

Have you ever needed a prayer answered and it seemed that either God was not listening or that he was being very slow in responding to your many urgent requests on the matter. Usually during this time we are asked to trust that God will provide. But to be honest, we admit that sometimes even that thought can be very difficult to do. Someone you love has been given so long to live. Or you desperately need a job so you can pay your bills. You pray and pray and pray... Many times instead of things getting better, the situation seems to get worst. Then at the midnight hour the need is met. They say that God is never too late and never too early. He is just on time. I believe this response is man's way of trying to explain the unexplainable. There are numerous scriptures in the Bible regarding answered prayer. But in regards to delayed answers, here is some food for thought:

1) *Have you ever considered that maybe all the players are not on the playfield yet*? The angel said, "Do not fear, Daniel, for from the first day that you

set your heart to understand, and humble yourself before God, your words were heard; and I have come because of your words. But the prince of the kingdom of Persia withstood me twenty-one days; and behold, Michael, one of the chief princes, came to help me" (Daniel 10:12-13).

2) *Maybe God is waiting for us to do something first*. Naaman, commander of the army of the king of Syria, was a leper. Elisha, the prophet of God, told Naaman to "Go and wash in the Jordan seven times, and your flesh will be restored to you, and you shall be clean" (2 Kings 5:10).

3) *This period of waiting tests our faith and trust in God*. The Book of Job tells of a man who lost his wealth, his family and his health. Through it all, Job remained faithful to God.

4) *Satan and his demon cohorts – the enemy and principalities in high places - try to stop the answers from reaching us*. The angel was bringing the answer to Daniel's prayer, but the prince of Persia withstood the angel for twenty-one days. (see Daniel 10:12-13). So we must never give up.

5) *Even though we do not see the answer, God is orchestrating the answer*. The army of Syria surrounded the army of Israel, outnumbering them. In response to Elisha's prayer for his servant, the Lord opened the eyes of the young man and he saw the mountain full of horses and chariots of fire all around Elisha. (see 2 Kings 6:15-17). God's provision could not be seen with the natural eye.

God watches over His children just like a parent would, only better. The Bible is filled with scriptures verifying that He loves us more than we can ever imagine or understand. God is omniscient. He knows the whole picture; therefore, as a trusting child of God we declare, "Father knows best." We rest as we wait for God's timing.

FOOD FOR THOUGHT: If we are a child of God, walking daily with Him, and obeying His statutes, we should be able to trust and lean on God for everything, big and small. We should know in our knower that God has heard us and He will answer our prayers.

I DON'T HAVE IDOLS IN MY LIFE (OR DO I)

SCRIPTURE:

And God spoke all these words, saying: "I am the Lord your God...You shall have no other gods before Me. You shall not make yourself a carved image... you shall not bow down to them nor serve them. For I, the Lord your God, am a jealous God, visiting the iniquity of the fathers upon the children to the third and fourth generations of those who hate Me, but showing mercy to thousands, to those who love Me and keep My commandments." (Exodus 20:1-6)

Idols? It may be easy to think we don't make carved images and worship them like the Israelites did when Moses was on the mountain receiving the Ten Commandments from God. Or, do we? An idol is anything that keeps us from serving God and obeying His Word.

Your response may be, "I go to church every Sunday. I don't steal. I don't commit murder. I obey the Ten Commandments."

I repeat. An idol is anything that we put before God. Let me share with you some of the idols that have been in my life...

God, I don't know if I can release my children to you. What if they need to go through a storm in their lives that will help them trust God in a deeper way? I don't know if I could watch them suffer.

God, I am very tired and I just want to crash on the couch and watch TV, where I don't have to do any thinking. I have had a very difficult day. I need to soothe my emotions with food, a cigarette, and maybe a couple of wine coolers. Maybe tomorrow I will feel fresher and then I will take time to read the Bible or pray.

Now that I have mentioned entertainment – what about the Soaps that we get involved in, the ungodly music that profanes God and the righteous way of living, or the football games that keep us from going to church on Sunday. Have I gone into meddling?

The alarm clock is ringing. I am going to hit the snooze button for the third time. I know I will be in a rush when I finally get out of bed and I won't have time to say, "Good Morning."

Lord, I know you asked me to give $20 to Ms. Smith, but I have been saving the money to buy me a dress.

Father, I don't want to forgive my husband for those horrible words he spoke to me in anger. I will not make the first move. He was wrong, so he has to be the first person to say, "I'm sorry."

There are a hundred more ways we put things before God, including our time, our families, and our jobs. If we are honest with ourselves, we will realize there are many things in our lives that have taken first place before God.

FOOD FOR THOUGHT: Father, I pray we will examine our hearts and seek the help of the Holy Spirit to show us what things we have placed first in our lives. Once we have realized that these things do exist, help us to break the hold they have in our lives. Thank you.

OUR COUNTRY – ONE NATION UNDER GOD

SCRIPTURE:

If my people who are called by My name will humble themselves, and pray and seek My face, and turn from their wicked ways, then I will hear from heaven and will forgive their sin and heal their land. (2 Chronicles 7:14)

We, the so called righteous people of God, have incorrectly pointed our fingers at the lost (people who do not know God and are not His children) and proclaimed that they are the wicked ones that God is talking about in 2 Chronicles 7:14. We have declared that if they turned from their sinful ways, then God would heal our land.

But the choice of a blessing or a curse was given to God's people (see Deuteronomy 28). We, God's children, are the ones who have sinned. We have been given God's Word, but we have not obeyed His Word. We have lowered our standards – the banner of covering over this nation. We have followed the dictates of our own hearts. We have sought out other "gods", such as money, possessions, careers (which none of these are bad in themselves), our own agenda, lusts of the flesh and our own assorted ways of perversions, and many more.

When the Israelites fell, it was because of the choices they made. They turned to "other gods" and followed the ways of the foreigners (those who did not follow after Jehovah God). In this country, we have done the same thing. We have accepted the world's way of thinking that is contrary to God's ways. It has slowly pervaded our thinking. We say that times have changed or that the Bible is not applicable for today. We were supposed to be an example to the lost – a light in a dark world. However, we have joined the darkness.

Father God, forgive us for we have sinned against you. We pray for your mercy. We don't want our country to go down in history as a country that "turned from God and did evil in His sight." As we, your people, humble ourselves, pray and seek your face, and turn from our wicked ways, hear our cries for mercy, forgive us and heal our land.

FOOD FOR THOUGHT: Our beloved country is at a crossroad. Which way will we choose? In Deuteronomy 30:19 God says, "I call heaven and earth as witnesses today against you, that I have set before you life and death, blessing and cursing: therefore, choose life that both you and your descendants may live." Father, we fall on our knees and seek your face. We repent of our wicked ways and we turn from them. We ask you to forgive us and heal our land.

BURDENS

SCRIPTURE:

Therefore humble yourselves under the mighty hand of God, that He may exalt you in due time, *casting all your care upon Him, for He cares for you.* (1Peter 5:6-7)

The burdens I carry are weights around my neck.
My shoulders sag under their heaviness.
My thoughts are crashing like a train wreck.
Soon I will drown under its insurmountable heaviness.

God, I give you the burdens of my heart.
They are too heavy for me to carry.
I should not have picked them up from the start.
But now they are yours to carry.

FOOD FOR THOUGHT: *Webster's Dictionary* defines <u>worry</u> as: to treat roughly, as with continual biting (a dog worrying a bone). When we worry, we allow the problem to continually bite at our thoughts. Father God, we pray that when a problem invades our lives, we will immediately cast the problem into your wise hands for you to take care of. We also ask for your help to leave the problem in your hands until it is solved.

MIRROR

SCRIPTURE:

Do you not know that you are the temple of God and that the Spirit of God dwells in you? (1 Corinthians 3:16)

A mirror in the bedroom, a mirror in the bathroom, a mirror in the hallway, and a mirror in the car.....there seemed to be a mirror everywhere. I used to avoid mirrors; I didn't want to see my reflection. Was I a painting gone astray? Was I a mistake that should have never been born? Was I afraid to face what I saw in the mirror? Yes. Yes. Oh, yes.

When I took time for a quick glance at my reflection, I saw insecurity, failure, pain, fear, and ugliness. When my gaze would catch the sadness in my eyes, the windows to the pain deep in my heart, I would quickly turn away.

But God was able to see pass the outer walls of my flesh and He was able to look deep into my heart. Only He knew how to heal the scars. Only He was able to exchange the ugliness for beauty. He gently scraped the mud that covered this vessel. Underneath it all, He was able to bring out the diamond that was inside.

Now when I look into a mirror, I can see pass the exterior. I see the princess that I have become. The light that is in me now shines out. All this is for the glory of God.

FOOD FOR THOUGHT: Like a mirror, our lives can reflect either good or evil. We pray that our lives reflect Jesus.

I WANT TO SAY NO

SCRIPTURE:

For I know that in me (that is, in my flesh) nothing good dwells; for to will is present with me, but how to perform what is good I do not find. For the good that I will to do, I do not do; but the evil I will not to do, that I practice. (Romans 7:18-19)

I want to say "No" to that bowl of double dip French vanilla ice cream covered with rich chocolate sauce, extra whip cream, lots of crushed walnuts, and the cherry on top. But the pull is so strong that I give into the desires of my flesh.

I want to say "No" to cigarettes, alcohol, drugs, or any addictions that have enticed, ensnared, and enslaved me. But the pull is so strong that I give into the desires of my flesh.

I want to say "No" to the sexual advances that don't rightfully belong to me. But the pull is so strong and I am unable to resist the desires of my flesh.

I want to say "No" to gossiping, backbiting, fowl language.....BUT

I want to say "No" but I seem to say "Yes" to the indulgence, the sin, the lust that entices and ensnares me.

Never give up. God doesn't. He has provided a way. "No temptation has overtaken you except such as is common to man; but God is faithful, who will not allow you to be tempted beyond what you are able, but with the temptation will also make the way of escape, that you may be able to bear it" (1 Corinthians 10:13).

The day we give up, sin wins. The answer is in renewing our mind through the Word and allowing the Word, along with the Holy Spirit to change us. We quote God's Word that declares we are "confident of this very thing, that He who has begun a good work in you will complete it until the day of Jesus Christ" (Philippians 1:6).

FOOD FOR THOUGHT: Father God, forgive me and bring deliverance to your child. Show me the way out. For you who have begun this good work in me are faithful to complete it by your own promise. Thank you, Lord.

HOLY SPIRIT STOPPED
SPEAKING TO ME

SCRIPTURE:

To You I will cry, O Lord my Rock: Do not be silent to me. (Psalm 28:1)

I will never forget the time when I did not hear the Holy Spirit speak to me – all because He said "NO" and I did not listen…

The first time the Holy Spirit spoke that word to me, it was very gently. But I ignored Him. My desires were stronger than obeying that still small voice I heard in my spirit. I gave into my desires. I made excuses that I was hurting and I needed the "fix" so that the pain would not be in the forefront. The temporary pleasure was for an instant. Pain returned and guilt became my companion.

I pledged not to give into my addiction. I was able to resist for awhile, but the pull was strong. I was not able to fight the desire that lured me away from the truth that God said I shouldn't. I convinced myself the pain was greater than I could handle. Again, I heard the Holy Spirit say, "No." This time it was a little louder, but I did not listen to His voice. As usual, my response to the pain gave into more guilt and condemnation, as if Satan was laughing at me. I begged God to forgive me.

This progression continued to happen until one day, in a clear loud voice, I heard the Holy Spirit say, "NO." I knew that if I made the wrong decision, I would not have close fellowship with Him. However, I still turned my back on God. I gave into the temporary pleasure of the fix, willing it to cover my pain. Following my previous path, I begged God to forgive me. This time, I did not hear God speak. The silence between me and the Holy Spirit was deafening. I made the choice. I chose "the sin of disobedience" over God.

Oh, how I missed the conversations with the Holy Spirit. I longed to hear His voice. I read my Bible. I prayed. I went to church. But my prayers seemed to bounce off the wall. I felt like the Israelites, who, because of their stiff-necked ways, walked in silence all those years, not hearing a word from God. Several months passed. I still did not hear anything. The emptiness inside me was like a deep cavern with no bottom. I remained on the path I knew best. I did not stop seeking God. Then one day, I heard the familiar voice of the Holy Spirit. He gently healed my broken heart and showed me the way out of my need for the wrong solution. I now lean on God for the answer. I have not been perfect, but I never again want to be without the voice of the Holy Spirit.

FOOD FOR THOUGHT: God created us to have intimate fellowship with Him. When we don't, there is emptiness which nothing else can satisfy. Forgive us when we are stiff-necked. Myself, personally, I don't ever want to experience that silence again.

PETER'S PRAYER

The Master once said to address You as "Father,"
And ask in His name as I pray.
I pray now, oh Father, thou who is worthy.
My future in Thine hands I lay.

The promise You'll send I await with full joy,
And anticipate to full degree.
This prayer I do beckon to Thee up above
To gain wholly the sweet victory.

Express in a twinkling the Truth of Thy Word,
And Thy will, not mine, to be done.
Help stand up my cross in the light of Thy Love,
And establish Thy goal through the Son.

Grant one thing, oh Father, to me 'afore I go;
Help sooth this my raw conscience sore.
Deliver me from the dark side of Thy cross
To live in Thy peace evermore.

By Ron Massman

PETER'S VICTORY

Here amid these many nations
I doth shout Thy Victory!
There between my veil of sorrow
By my side Thy Spirit be.

From my lips Thy words doth tumble.
In my mind Thy Truth unfolds.
Energized by Thy pure power,
Grace for all Thine own bestows.

Rocks and trees and sparrows hold
Such secrets as my soul doth see.
Visions of a love sustaining,
Exposing this: Thy mystery.

Future whims, they bring no comfort,
In Thy hands their value weigh.
Specters, visions, foolish, trouble,
When compared to present day.

Here a longing host awaits me,
Sent by Thine own Spirit's throng.
Fill me with my day of power,
From Thy present, perfect song.

Laid beneath cold, blackened embers
Rests deep a life which shadowed Thee.
Mirrored at the foot of Calvary,
Glows a cross of victory.

By Ron Massman

THE BLANKET

SCRIPTURE:

And above all things have fervent love for one another, for love will cover a multitude of sins. (1 Peter 4:8)

There is nothing like a thick, warm blanket on a cold winter night. The temperature outside is twenty degrees below zero, while inside the house the temperature is sixty-eight. Snow has covered the land with a thick white blanket. The wind is blowing, causing the trees to speak as if shivering. But when my warm, fuzzy blanket covers me, I don't feel the cold. The blanket protects me from the harshness that is raging war outside my house.

The blood of Jesus covers us like a blanket. It keeps the penalty for our sins away from us. We do not have to pay the price of eternal damnation (apart from God). We have been set free. The harshness of sin may be waging war, but we can speak the blood of Jesus over our lives. It protects us from Satan. It helps us feel safe and secure.

As stated in 1 Peter 4:8, love covers a multitude of sins. The love of God provided His son, Jesus, as a free gift to us so we do not have to live in the torment that sin brings. When we ask Jesus into our hearts, the love of God covers our sins like a blanket. When

God looks at us, He does not see our sins. He sees the righteousness of Jesus.

God set an example for the way we should live. God gave us two commandments. In Matthew 22:37-40, Jesus said, "You shall love the Lord your God with all your heart, with all your soul, and with all your mind. This is the first and great commandment. And the second is like it: You shall love your neighbor as yourself. On these two commandments hang all the Law and the Prophets." So when someone does something wrong, we should give them the blanket of love that covers a multitude of sins.

FOOD FOR THOUGHT: Father, I pray that we will love others as you loved us. I pray that we will forgive others as you forgave us. Love heals wounds. I pray that we will give to the hurting the blanket of love that protects and keeps them safe from the evil one.

PORTRAIT OF GOD
(Character of God)

SCRIPTURE:

If you had known Me, you would have known My Father also; and from now on you know Him and have seen Him. (John 14:7)

According to the Bible, no one has seen God, but we can know the character of God. Common phrases, such as "like father, like son" or "spitting image", echo the idea that we can know God by looking at Jesus.

Galatians 5:22-23 lists the fruits of the Holy Spirit: love, joy, peace, longsuffering, kindness, goodness, faithfulness, gentleness and self-control. Jesus, who is part of the trinity (God the Father, Jesus the Son, and the Holy Spirit), is a conduit of these characteristics. Subsequently, we can assume that God likewise possesses these qualities.

We know God so loved the world that He sent His only Son to Earth (see John 3:16, 17). Can you imagine what it would take to let your only child die for another? I don't think I could do it. But God did. God's love is beyond anything we can comprehend.

Like His Father, Jesus was moved with compassion. According to Matthew 4:23, "Jesus went about all Galilee, teaching in their synagogues, preaching the gospel of the kingdom, and healing all kinds of sickness and all kinds of disease among the people." In Luke 19:41 we see Jesus weeping over the city of Jerusalem.

While Jesus walked the dusty roads here on Earth, He visited all sorts of people: lepers, blind men, adulterers, tax collectors, demon-possessed people, a dead man whom He brought back to life, rulers, the rich, the poor, and the sick. The Jewish leaders accused Jesus of associating with the wrong people. When they questioned Jesus concerning this matter, Jesus responded, "Those who are well have no need of a physician, but those who are sick" (Matthew 9:12). If Jesus was concerned about the sick, the hurting, and the sinful and He did only what His Father wanted Him to do, again we can assume that God is concerned about the sick, hurting, and sinful also.

Matthew 19:13-14 depicts Jesus' love for children. Little children were brought to Jesus so He could lay hands on them and pray. When the disciples rebuked them, Jesus said, "Let the little children come to Me, and do not forbid them; for of such is the kingdom of heaven."

Jesus displayed His power over the physical realm when He rebuked the storm and then there was a calm (see Matthew 8:26), spoke to the fig tree and it withered (see Matthew 21:19), and walked on water (see Matthew 14:25).

Jesus was a servant. He "made Himself of no reputation, taking the form of a bondservant, and coming in the likeness of men" (Philippians 2:7).

Jesus stated He is our friend. "Greater love has no man than this, than to lay down one's life for His friends" (John 15:13).

In John 10:14 Jesus declared, "I am the good shepherd, and I know My sheep, and am known by My own." If you study the duties of a good shepherd, you will discover that the shepherd knows his flock, he protects them from harm, and he provides for them.

One of the greatest gifts a person can give another is to forgive that person, whether they deserve it or not. On the cross, Jesus said, "Father, forgive them for they do not know what they do" (Luke 23:34). Jesus forgave them for beating Him, mocking Him, spitting on Him, cursing Him, denying Him, and crucifying Him.

As we look at the life of Jesus, we can see the character of God, who is the ultimate picture of love.

FOOD FOR THOUGHT: I pray we will reflect the character of God. We learn God's character when we study the life of Jesus and what He did here on Earth.

THE NAMES OF GOD

SCRIPTURES:

He raised Him from the dead and seated Him at His right hand in the heavenly places, far above all principality and power and might and dominion, and every name that is named, not only in this age but also in that which is to come. And He put all things under His feet, and gave Him to be head over all things to the church. (Ephesians 1:20-22)

Therefore God also has highly exalted Him and given Him the name which is above every name, that at the name of Jesus every knee should bow, of those in Heaven, and of those on Earth, and of those under the Earth, and that every tongue should confess that Jesus Christ is Lord, to the glory of God the Father. (Philippians 2:9-11)

Below I have listed a few of the names of God that I found by cross referencing between the names of God I heard in church, the Bible and *Strong's Exhaustive Concordance of the Bible* (see Appendix):

JEHOVAH: The *Lord* (see Genesis 6:3).
YAHWEH: *I am* that I am (see Exodus 3:14).
EL OHIM: He is the *Most High God* (see Genesis 1:1).
JEHOVAH-ROI: He is my *Shepherd*, the one who protects me (see Psalm 23:1).

JEHOVAH-JIREH: He is my *provider* (see Genesis 22:8).

JEHOVAH-ADONAI: He is my *Sovereign Lord* (see Psalm 97:5).

JEHOVAH-SHALOM: He is my *peace* (see Judges 6:24).

JEHOVAH-ROPHE: He is my *healer*, the One who makes me whole (see Isaiah 53:5).

JEHOVAH-TSIDKENU: He is my *righteousness* (see Jeremiah 23:5).

JEHOVAH-SHAMMAH: He is always with me; Jehovah is *there* (see Ezekiel 48:35).

JEHOVAH-NISSI: He is my *banner* (see Exodus 17:15).

JEHOVAH-MEKADDESH: He *sanctifies* me (see Leviticus 20:8).

JEHOVAH-EL SHADDAI: He is God *Almighty* (see Genesis 17:1).

ABBA: *Father* (see Galatians 4:6).

There are many more names that represent the character of God, and His son Jesus. God has exalted the name of Jesus above all names, including cancer, depression, and poverty. Every name has to bow to the name of Jesus.

FOOD FOR THOUGHT: One time during worship service, I called out YESHUA. When I repeated YESHUA, I inadvertently said "YES YOU ARE, my everything," which is very true.

DISCIPLE

To each and every one of us,
There comes a time, you see,
A chance of making Jesus
First and placed upon His tree.

Though wild by nature we reside in
Him whose Grace we seek.
Thus grafted in, what joy we have;
We know that Grace we'll keep.

As sap He's there to freely flow
And fill us every day;
His Holy Spirit builds us up
To His more perfect way.

As leaves we open to the light
Our minds to thoughts of You;
And grow much stronger every day
As we, oh, Lord, are true.

Up we grow as we reach out,
For on the earth we'll stay,
Until we meet you in the air,
That day…Oh glorious day!

But until then our tree we'll bear,
Disciples we will be,
For long ago You died for us,
You are our destiny.

By Ron Massman

I CAN BECAUSE OF JESUS

SCRIPTURE:

Take therefore no thought for the morrow; for the morrow shall take thought for the things of itself. Sufficient unto the day is the evil thereof. (Matthew 6:34 King James Version)

Sometimes life seems so overwhelming, especially when I am trying to overcome a habit, accomplish a project, or just dealing with the everyday problems of life. My past reminds me of my failures, blaring in my mind that I should bow my head down to its hold over me. Or I may look at the future as an unknown mountain that I do not know how to climb, succumbing to the fear that I cannot do it. Both situations are incongruent with God's Word and will for my life. God reminds me I need to put my past in the past, placing it under the blood of Jesus. He exhorts me not to worry about the future because it has not come yet. I have today.

With my heart and mouth I declare in a bold fashion that I can handle the challenges of today. I agree with the Word of God which tells me who I am in Him. I can do all things with His help. I am redeemed from the curse. I am daily changed from glory to glory into His image. I am the head and not the tail. I am an overcomer. I have the wisdom of God to teach me. I have the mind of Christ. I am filled with the Holy Spirit who guides me. I am a conqueror in Christ Jesus. The confirming words of who I am in Christ Jesus, because of the cross, go on and on. As I line myself up with the image God has of me, my demeanor is lifted up. I can take that one step forward, knowing that God is with me to help me accomplish that which He has ordained for me to do. Again, I say, I CAN handle the challenges of today.

This reminds me of the children's story of the little engine trying to climb a treacherous hill to reach its destination. As he climbed the steep hill, he kept saying, "I think I can. I think I can. I think I can." My twist to this story is to say, "I know I can. I know I can. I know I can. All because of Jesus."

FOOD FOR THOUGHT: Father God, help us to take it one day at a time, not looking at our failures or looking forward with worry. We trust you to help us through this day.

GOD HAS PREPARED A TABLE

SCRIPTURE:

You prepare a table before me in the presence of my enemies. (Psalm 23:5)

I have prepared a table for you – all you could possibly need is on that table. There is salvation, healing, deliverance, peace, love, joy, faithfulness, protection, guidance, friendship, plus many more good things – everything you need to live a victorious life here on Earth.

Just like the table you prepare for yourselves (which may include meat, potatoes, vegetables, bread, fruit, nuts, condiments, milk, and desserts), you must partake of the meal. For example, even though vegetables are on the table, you may choose not to eat them. When you don't eat the vegetables, you are denying yourself the benefits they can give your body. Eventually, you could suffer the consequences of not eating the very food your bodies require to live a healthy life.

The same occurs at My table. Even though salvation has been prepared for everyone, a person may choose not to accept salvation. You may decide not to partake of the deliverance that I have provided. Or you could choose not to ask for My help in time of trouble. I have provided everything you need; however, the choices are yours.

FOOD FOR THOUGHT: We want to partake of everything that God has prepared for us. We are not selective eaters.

STIR THE WATERS

SCRIPTURE:

Again He said to me [Ezekiel], "Prophesy to these bones, and say to them 'O dry bones, hear the word of the Lord! 'Thus says the Lord God to these Bones: "Surely I will cause breath to enter into you, and you shall live. I will put sinews on you and bring flesh upon you, cover you with skin and put breath in you; and you shall live. Then you shall know that I am the Lord." ' " (Ezekiel 37:4-6)

The air is stagnant; there is no breeze.
The trees are silent; there is no wind.
The sky is without clouds; there is no rain.
The ground is dry; there is no water.

My Spirit is quiet; there is no sound of God's voice.
My faith is lacking; there is no victory.

Stir the waters.
Again I say, stir the waters before it is too late.
Stir the waters; read and speak the Word of God.
Stir the waters; sing praises to the King of Kings.
Stir the waters; spend time with the giver of life.

I feel a breeze; the air is fresh again.
The wind is blowing; the trees speak again.
Rain drops are falling; the ground becomes moist.
The sky is filled with clouds; the rain is pouring down.

The waters have been stirred.
I hear the voice of my Savior.
The blessings come.

FOOD FOR THOUGHT: When we don't take time to worship God, read the Bible, pray, and go to Church, we become dry in our spirit. I pray that each day we will choose to spend time with God.

OUR WAY OR GOD'S WAY

SCRIPTURE:

"For My thoughts are not your thoughts, nor are your ways My ways," says the Lord. "For as the heavens are higher than the earth, so are My ways higher than your ways, and my thoughts than your thoughts." (Isaiah 55:8, 9)

In Chapter 6 of 2 Samuel, we have the story about David trying to bring the Ark back to Jerusalem. In their enthusiasm, they neglected to seek God first regarding the requirements of transporting the Ark. David selected choice men of Israel. They set the Ark on a new cart and proceeded on their way. The story goes on to explain that Uzzah put his hand out to keep the Ark from falling when the oxen stumbled. Immediately, Uzzah died.

When first reading this, I felt God was so unfair. Later, I learned that God had previously stated the correct requirements for transporting the Ark. According to Numbers 4:15 and 7:9, the sons of Kohath, who were in charge of the holy things, were to carry the ark on their shoulders. David did not seek God first. He didn't research God's established Word on the subject (see 1 Chronicles15:13). He built a new cart and he selected choice men of Israel.

Many things are harmful for us in our lives. They may look good on the outside, but if we say "Yes" to them, we may regret our decision.

We may not always understand God's ways. We see our lives with a finite mind. God is omniscient; therefore, He knows all and He knows the best way. When we have a problem or a decision to make, we need to go to God first. We can pray, search His Word, and listen to the Holy Spirit speak to our spirit that lives in us. Do we listen to God with the ears of the flesh (our desires or worldly mind), or do we listen to God with our spiritual ears?

FOOD FOR THOUGHT: Father, we pray we will seek you first with our daily decisions and problems. We need to let go of the reins of our lives and trust you as you guide us down the right path.

WHEN I AM - YOU ARE

SCRIPTURE:

I sought the Lord, and He heard me, and delivered me from all my fears. (Psalm 34:4)

When I am down, you lift me up.

When I succeed, you celebrate with me.

When I have a need, you provide.

When I make a mistake, you forgive. You brush the dust off me and tell me to try again.

When tears of pain and rejection flow from my eyes, you catch them and put them in a bottle, transforming them into an aromatic fragrance of life.

When I am alone, you lean close so I can hear your heart beat and feel the touch of your presence.

When I am stumped by a problem, your wisdom shines forth with the solution.

When I am ashamed and disgusted with myself, you show me how much you love me.

When the enemy rejoices that he is going to destroy me, you remind me that you are greater than the foe and that I win.

When I am afraid of the darkness that surrounds me, you turn the light on and let me see your glorious face.

When I am overwhelmed with life, you step into my day, bringing rest and peace.

When sickness carries me to near death, your Word restores me to health, because it was not my appointed time.

When my heart aches for the loss of a loved one, you remind me that grief is for a season, and joy comes in the morning.

When I get angry and full of pride, you chasten me with your silence. Then I repent and I am ready to hear and obey your voice.

When I am stiff-necked and slow to respond to your voice, you are patient with me. You never give up on me.

When I am hungry and thirsty for righteousness, you fill me.

When I enjoy the simple things of life, I am told that you created them for my pleasure.

When you show me your masterpiece of creation, I humble myself to your Lordship.

FOOD FOR THOUGHT: I pray that in every circumstance we face in life, we will come to you first. You are the answer to every aspect of life. We don't face each day by ourselves. You are always with us.

REVERENTIAL FEAR OF GOD

SCRIPTURES:

The fear of the Lord is the beginning of wisdom. (Psalm 111:10; Proverbs 9:10)

The fear of the Lord is the beginning of knowledge. (Proverbs 1:7)

I appreciate certain things from my Catholic upbringing. The reverential fear of God I sensed while attending mass and the disciplined commitment of being in Church every Sunday are a few. That fear and respect is still part of my life. I no longer see God as only a disciplinarian who is ready to knock me down when I make a mistake. I perceive God as a loving father who is very much concerned about my well-being.

Sometimes we associate fear with negative connotations. If we are afraid, we flinch or hide from the one who is causing the fear. With God, we need a fear that does not cause us to hide from Him, but to seek God with everything we have. I believe that with God, we need a reverential fear that will cause us to respect God and to know He can and He will do what He has promised in His Word. We need to "know that we know that we know in our knower" that His word is the ultimate truth and we should base everything we do around His Word. The spiritual arena is greater than our natural-physical sur-roundings we live in each day ("He who is in you is greater than he who is in the world" – 1 John 4:4). We should be more concerned about rejecting God than rejecting man. Sometimes we are more afraid of offending man than we are of offending God.

In a twinkling of an eye God can speak some-thing into existence. He divided the Red Sea and the Jordan River for the Israelites. He destroyed nations because they worshipped other gods. When God speaks, all of Heaven and Earth will bow to Him, including Satan. There is no one that is greater than God, who is the creator of the universe.

We can come to God with the knowledge He is the "Big Daddy." We have the promises of God to help us live a blessed life, not to just survive but to be victorious in our walk on Earth. We can take His promises "to the bank." We must be careful not to be presumptuous of God. We humble ourselves before the One who has supreme wisdom and knowledge on how to live. Let us be in awe of God. Let us honor Him with reverential fear.

FOOD FOR THOUGHT: Father God, we don't want to be irreverent in our attitude toward you. We humble ourselves before you, not asking anything at this moment, but just to honor you with our praise, knowing that without you we could not stand against the storms of life. We know you are all powerful and your Word is truth. You say that we can come boldly into the throne of grace (see Hebrews 4:16), so we know that you don't want us to hide from you.

WORTHY

Worthy art thou, oh great Saviour of mine,
Worthy art thou who wast slain;
Glory and honor and blessing be Thine,
Praise to Thy glorious name!

Yea worthy of praise, sing ye heavens above,
Is the Lamb through whom all blessings flow;
Thy majesty set for all ages to love
And abide in clay hearts down below!

Worthy to know, Thy Word boldly proclaims,
Is Thy law which my opened eyes see;
Guilty was I till Thou unlocked my chains,
On that day that Thou set my life free!

Bountiful mercies Thou send by Thy Dove,
Grace measured by endless degree;
Visions of rapture Thou bought by Thy Love,
Thy blessed assurance for me!

By Ron Massman

JESUS VALIDATES ME

SCRIPTURE:

The Spirit Himself bears witness with our spirit that we are children of God, and if children, then heirs – heirs of God and joint heirs with Christ. (Romans 8:16, 17a)

I don't have to prove anything to Jesus.
Winner or loser, champion or recluse;
He is no respecter of persons.
Jesus died for me, no matter who I was.

I don't have to buy entrance to Heaven;
It is a free gift.
I only have to say "Yes".

I don't have to live in the fanciest home,
To prove that I am somebody special.
I am loved by the creator of the universe.

I don't have to be Number One.
There is only one person that fulfills that position.
He is the I Am, the Alpha and the Omega.

I don't have to be validated by a person.
Legally I am a child of God,
All because of the blood of Jesus.
Jesus validates me.

FOOD FOR THOUGHT: Our self-esteem, our security, our purpose is based on the love of God and our walk with Him.

BE STILL AND HEAR GOD SPEAK

SCRIPTURES:

Be still and know that I am God. (Psalm 46:10)

And Moses said to them, "Stand still, that I may hear what the Lord will command concerning you." (Numbers 9:8)

It is in the quiet times when I put aside the rush of the day that I can hear God speak to my heart. I turn the television off, I close the door to the outside world, and I take time to tell my heavenly Father I want to spend time with Him. I express my love to Him in many ways – sometimes with words of thanks, sometimes with a song, or sometimes just being quiet and letting Him know that He is more important to me than the breath I take. I speak. I become quiet and listen. Yes. I sense He is talking. I wait a little longer, resting in His presence. Then I hear the words of my heavenly Father drop into my spirit. Those few words speak volumes to me, just what I needed for that moment.

Then there are times, right in the middle of the madness of life, I take five minutes and turn the noise off. I tell God that I love him. Just those few minutes can mean so much, as if I received a high-five from God. I am more refreshed. Just what I needed to go on.

Morning, noon, or night – in the bathtub, washing my face, driving the car, eating my food – all of these represent opportunities to take time from a busy schedule (that we created) and just say "Hi" to God. This lets Him know we realize we cannot (don't want to) go through the day without Him. During those few quiet moments, we can hear from God, because He desires to speak to His children. He is just waiting for someone to turn their ears in His direction.

FOOD FOR THOUGHT: Father, even if it is only for a few seconds, I pray we will take time to listen to you speak to us. Those moments we spend together gives us strength to go on.

HOW DEEP IS THE RIVER FLOWING?

SCRIPTURE:

Then he brought me back to the door of the temple; and there was water, flowing from under the threshold of the temple toward the east...brought me through the waters; the water came up to my knees... and he brought me through, the water came up to my waist...again it was a river that I could not cross; for the water was too deep, water in which one must swim, a river that could not be crossed...and it shall be that every living thing that moves, wherever the rivers go, will live. (Ezekiel 47:1, 4-5, 9)

The river is flowing, but I don't want to get wet. I gingerly position one foot at the edge of the river; the water is cold to the touch. I decide to maintain control of my life by pulling my foot out of the water.

The river is flowing; I decide to wade in a little further. This time the water is to my knees. Since my feet are touching the ground, I still hold the reins of my life.

The river is flowing; I walk in a little further. This time the water is up to my waste. I feel my body sway a little by the force of the current. I don't know if I am ready to let God have sovereign dominion over my life. I am secure in the fact that my feet are still touching the ground.

219

The river is flowing; I can't see my feet. The water is splashing around my neck. I almost lose my balance. Fear wants to say that I shouldn't go any further, but the current of my desire to go deeper into the presence of God is stronger.

The river is flowing. Where will it take me? I no longer can touch the ground. I no longer have control. The current is very strong. My life is completely in the hands of God. He is my Master.

FOOD FOR THOUGHT: I desire to jump into the deepest part of the river where I no longer have control of my life. I know that in your presence is life, fuller than I can imagine.

THE STORM

SCRIPTURE:

Now when they had left the multitude, they took Him along in the boat as He was. And other little boats were also with Him. And a great windstorm arose, and the waves beat into the boat, so that it was already filling. But He was in the stern, asleep on a pillow. And they awoke Him and said to Him, "Teacher, do You not care that we are perishing?" Then He arose and rebuked the wind, and said to the sea, "Peace, be still!" And the wind ceased and there was a great calm. (Mark 4:36-39)

The storms came raging across the gulf with a flurry.
Destruction and death were their names.
Homes and lives became no more under their furry.
Only debris would remain.

The storm knocked at our door,
Bringing desolation wherever it roamed.
When we believed we couldn't handle any more,
The fierce storm continued, so that we moaned.

Each storm brought the wind and rain;
The high waves of despair showed no mercy.
In the darkness, we thought the storm would remain.
The results of the damage caused us to worry.

The storm of death came like a surprise.
When it departed, our hearts were sunken.
The storm took our joy as a prize.
The aftermath left our lives broken.

In the end, we had only one choice;
The storm rampaged our land.
We cried out to God with a loud voice;
"By the grace of God we stand."

FOOD FOR THOUGHT: The storms of life have whipped at each and every one of us at one time or another. In the midst of the storms, we call out to the only person who can calm the storms. His name is Jesus.

A LETTER TO GOD

SCRIPTURE:

But seek first the kingdom of God and His righteousness, and all these things shall be added to you. (Matthew 6:33)

Dear God,

Life has been hectic lately. I have been working overtime. When I come home I am faced with the responsibilities of the house and the children. At the end of the day, I am so tired. I lay my head down to sleep, realizing I have not spent any time with you today. I hope I can find time tomorrow.

The bills have piled up and I don't see an end to the stack. When the phone rings, I am afraid to answer. It might be a bill collector with harassing words. So please understand why I didn't tithe this month. I just don't have enough money to pay both the bills and the tithe. You understand, don't you?

Before I forget, I want to thank you for this beautiful home. I know the payments are a little higher than I can afford. But I am reaching for the American dream. I work very hard. I deserve this fancy house. And of course, your Word says you will supply all our needs.

God, you won't believe what I encountered today. On the way to work, I saw a homeless man lying on the street. There was a sign beside him, which read: "I have lost my home and my family. Can you help me? I will work for food." I can't believe the audacity of that man to ask for help. He needs to get his lazy self up off the sidewalk and find a job. I am not going to waste my hard earned money on him.

My children show no respect. They should understand I am working hard so that I can give them everything they want. I can't help it that I don't have time to spend with them. We hardly communicate anymore. I don't know what to do.

By the way, what right does the Pastor have to speak on personal matters, such as drinking, gambling, lusts of the flesh and what we watch on television? I think he has entered the area of meddling. Maybe it is time I find a new church, one that is more in tune with the times.

Woe to me. The long hours at work, the stress of the job and the lack of sleep have finally taken its toll on my body. The doctors have informed me that if I don't change my lifestyle, my heart will not last much longer. Father God, I am scared and I don't know what to do.

I am writing this letter to you. I hope I hear a response soon. Lately I have not been hearing your voice very clearly.

Your desperate child

FOOD FOR THOUGHT: Father God, forgive us. We have become so busy with our daily lives that we have slowly slipped in to the same thinking as the world. We need to have Jehovah God (Our Provider) first place in our lives. Restore that first love of when we first made you our Lord and Savior.

GOD'S RESPONSE TO LETTER

SCRIPTURE:

Ask, and it will be given to you, seek, and you will find, knock, and it will be opened to you. (Matthew 7:7)

Dear Child,

I love you more than you can imagine. I have been waiting with anticipation to hear from you. I missed our daily conversations we used to have. Sadly, you have chosen to follow the dictates of your own heart. You have put me last in your life. Repeatedly, my Word explains that if you diligently seek me, obey my voice, heed the commandments which I have given you, then I will bless you (see Exodus 15:26 and Deuteronomy 28:1-14).

I am the Lord who provides your needs. Promises are based on conditions. I explained in my Word that you need to bring the tithes and offerings into the storehouse. Then I will open up the windows of heaven and pour out a blessing that you would not have room to contain it. I want you to try me and prove me. I will rebuke the devourer off your finances for your sake (see Malachi 3:10, 11).

I know your needs before you are aware of them. But you need to seek me first. If you are faithful in the little things, then I can give you more (see Luke

16:10). I can bless you with the things you desire if you are a good steward of your money and time. Remember, if you abide in me and my words abide in you, your desires will line up with the word of God. Then whatever you ask, it shall be done (see John 15:7).

I have called my children to be servants to the needy and the hurting. Jesus shared this principle with His disciples: when you help the least of my brethren, you are doing it unto me (see Matthew 25:34-46). I watch my children to see if they have a passion for the hurting. This pleases me, and I will bless those who bless others.

Pastors, like the "Good Shepherd," are required to feed and nourish my sheep. Pastors are held accountable for any false doctrine that leads God's children astray (see Ezekiel 34:1-10). If the words of your pastor line up with the Bible, you need to listen.

I know you want to be a good parent. But your children need your attention more than material things. If you are not there for them, they will seek what they need from other people. It is never too late to turn the situation around. As you re-establish a relationship with your children, I will help you.

Your heart. I have good plans for your life (see Jeremiah 29:11). But if you don't take care of your body the way you should, these plans will not come to pass. Stress comes when you worry, work too hard, and don't receive the rest your body needs. Give your cares to me (see 1 Peter 5:7). Activate the healing power by disciplining your body with correct eating habits, with exercise, and with sleep. Your body can be restored to health.

Come to me with your burdens and I will give you rest. My mercy and compassion never fade. I desire to restore your health, provide for you, and heal your wounds. But you must put me first in your life. I am as close to you as a heartbeat. Trust me and I will take care of you.

Your loving Father, God

FOOD FOR THOUGHT: God wants to bless His people. He is the "Good Shepherd." As indicated in Luke 11:13, if we, who are evil, know how to give good gifts to our children, how much more will our heavenly Father want to give good gifts to us.

THE PRESENCE OF GOD

SCRIPTURE:

Oh, taste and see that the Lord is good, blessed is the man who trusts in Him. (Psalm 34:8)

I fall on my knees with a contrite and broken heart. What I desire more than anything in this world is to know you, walk with you, talk with you, and please you. I hunger for your touch. I push away anything that keeps me from enjoying your presence. You have created in me a passion to seek you. Nothing else on earth will satisfy.

I wake up in the morning and you are the first thought on my mind. As I go through the day, I talk to you about anything and everything. When I go to bed at night, I close my eyes thinking about you. You have created in me a passion to seek you. Nothing else on earth will satisfy.

You have walked with me through the storms of life and you have proven to me that you love me – my life is safe in your hands. There were times I did not know you were there; nevertheless, you were by my side. You have held me up when the raging rivers threatened to drown me. You have created in me a passion to seek you. Nothing else on earth will satisfy.

I hear you calling my name. I come a running into the arms of a loving Father. I give you my all.

In your presence, I am lost for words. All I can do is fall on my knees and worship you. You have created in me a passion to seek you. Nothing else on earth will satisfy.

FOOD FOR THOUGHT: Father, you have created in us a "hole" that can only be filled by you. I pray that each person will comprehend what it is like to know the love of God. I pray that each person will seek you with everything they have. When they do, I know you will fill it with your presence that is indescribable.

TWILIGHT AWAKENING

Fear beckons, thoughts arise.
Predictably, the first few moments of doubt
Create dark illusions of life once lived
In the gray area of compromise.

Enter you, Jesus. Because your work is complete
I have your peace that sustains me.
Moment by moment your rest prevails.
Your presence is sure from my rising up to my
lying down.

By your grace fear, feebleness and doubt
Are replaced by your Love and your Strength.
Can a Love so pure bear even
One impure thought?
Can He who lives in me impart
The slightest hint of darkness?

In the twilight of my journey
I claim your Lamp for my feet,
That I may stay on the path of righteousness.
Thoughts some remind of past failures;
I proclaim your light to preserve
Integrity the world knows not.

Yes Jesus, from darkness you deliver me
To the light of hope
That shines forth on my soul.
Earnest prayers of a grateful heart
Give way to a renewed life of faith;
You are faithful!

Your abundance overflows exceedingly
To every dark and unseen corner of the path
You have chosen for me.
Knowing this:
I covet not your reward,
But claim your sustaining grace.
I boast not your gifts,
Save their hope to a dying world.
I praise not our provision
Lest it glorifies you;
Lord of my life!

Having sustained me
Through the dark days of my youth,
May my life now reflect
A sacrifice of praise!

Amen! Lord, you are worthy of praise.

By Ron Massman

AM I A TRUE FRIEND?

SCRIPTURE:

No longer do I call you servants, for a servant does not know what his master is doing, but I have called you friends, for all things that I heard from My Father I have made known to you. (John 15:15)

I have a friend who is closer than a sister. She is always there whenever I need her. She thinks it nothing to change her plans so she can be with me during a crisis. She stands by me through thick or thin, good times and bad times. I have poured out the secrets of my heart and they are safe with her. When she calls, my countenance is uplifted with encouragement. I enjoy spending time with her. Our hearts are knitted together with a strong bond of love. My friend is a gift from God.

I also have a very special friend. His name is Jesus. His friendship is more precious to me than gold. He is a friend who sticks closer than a brother. He says "I will never leave you nor forsake you" (Hebrews 13:5). He is the lifter of my head, my fortress, and my strong tower. His counsel is always correct. His Word is trustworthy. He brings me immeasurable love, peace beyond human understanding, and joy unspeakable. Jesus laid His life down for me – this is the ultimate gift of a friend.

This leads to the million-dollar question – am I a true friend to others? Am I a friend to Jesus? Do I hear His voice? Do I hesitate when He calls? Do I always stand by Him, or do I serve Him when it is only convenient for me? Do I listen to His words and keep them safely in my heart? Do I get excited in His presence? Do I enjoy spending time with Jesus? Am I willing to help others as Jesus would? Am I trustworthy? Jesus calls me friend. Do I reciprocate the friendship? I am blessed with friends, but am I a true friend?

FOOD FOR THOUGHT: The Word of God says that Jesus calls us friend. We need to ask ourselves, "Am I a true friend?" If not, we need to learn how to reciprocate Jesus' friendship. It starts by spending time with Him and reading His Word, which leads us to know what pleases Him and how to serve Him. In actuality, we receive more from Jesus than we can ever give back to Him.

A WOUNDED HEART
A WOUNDED SOUL RESTORED

SCRIPTURE:

The Spirit of the Lord God is upon Me, because the Lord has anointed Me to preach good tidings to the poor; He has sent Me to heal the brokenhearted, to proclaim liberty to the captives, and the opening of the prison to those who are bound; to proclaim the acceptable year of the Lord, and the day of vengeance of our God; to comfort all who mourn, to console those who mourn in Zion, to give them beauty for ashes, the oil of joy for mourning, the garment of praise for the spirit of heaviness; that they may be called trees of righteousness, the planting of the Lord, that He may be glorified. (Isaiah 61:1-3)

PART ONE: A WOUNDED HEART

This heart I hold tight within,
Enclosed by walls that cannot be penetrated.
Being hurt once, I give reason to naivety.
Hurt twice, I am convinced I was deceived.
Third time around, hope displaced foolishness.

This heart will not be given away again.
The door to my heart has been sealed shut.
The key has been thrown into the deepest ocean.
The location of its deposit will be forgotten.

This heart is protected by distance.
No one will be able to enter in.
I will not let it feel again.
It will be safer this way.
I will not take the chance of being hurt again.

This heart becomes cold, hard and dried up,
Since warmth is not let in to bring life.
The locked door and the walls around it
Have accomplished their purpose.

This heart of mine has been broken.
The scars are visible to anyone who looks.
The scar tissue has dangerously built up,
Creating blockage, producing death.

PART TWO: A WOUNDED SOUL RESTORED

She walks into a room with her eyes looking down.
Her countenance reveals a broken heart.
She avoids making contact with anyone,
Skirting the outside of the crowd,
Hoping to be ignored.

An elderly woman slowly approaches this wounded
soul, hoping not to push the young lady away.
She lovingly reaches out a hand,
Not too invasive or demanding,
But with the intention to break the distance.

The young lady is trapped.
The wall behind her gives her no place to run.
With every fiber in her body,
She screams, NO.
But she stands still, awaiting the encounter.

The elderly lady knows this wounded soul
Needs special handling.
She speaks in a gentle, but unwavering voice;
"Welcome, God loves you."

On return visits to this small church,
The elderly lady persistently sought her out.
Each encounter became easier to face.
First it was the welcoming words,
Then the gentle handshake,
Which led to the unavoidable hug.

Each hug tore at the walls around her heart.
The warm and gentle touch of another caring soul
Melted the false protection she had built up.
Healing words were salve to her broken heart,
Restoring life of a precious soul.

The process was slow.
There were times she wanted to return
To her secure walls of safety.
But each baby step
Brought joy back into her heart.

Today, she no longer hides from people.
Each morning brings anticipation,
Knowing she will encounter hurting people.
She has been given the gift of love,
Which in return she is now able to give to others.

(In remembrance of Sister Morgan, who now sees her Jesus face to face.)

FOOD FOR THOUGHT: Father, your Word says you are no respecter of persons (see Acts 10:34). What you did for me, you can do for whosoever calls on your name. We pray for the brokenhearted, that they will reach out to Jehovah God, the only one who can heal and restore their broken hearts.

PROVERB 31 WOMAN

SCRIPTURE:

Honor your father and your mother, as the Lord your God has commanded you, that your days may be long, and that it may be well with you in the land which the Lord your God is giving you. (Deuteronomy 5:16)

She gave birth to me when she was very young and uncertain if she was ready for the challenge of a little one. But she accepted her role. She nurtured me with food of life, love, and security of a cozy home.

I saw a woman who was dedicated and loyal to her husband. She was his helpmate. I witnessed a love and a bond that grew between them. They started as two separate people, and then they became one.

Her hands were never idle. Every day of the week she kept her routine. Monday was washday. On Tuesday, she ironed. Wednesday culminated in mending. Thursday, she made sure the house was spotless. Friday was spent at the grocery store. On Saturday, she cooked the pastries that teased our appetites. On Sunday, she was in church giving thanks to God for His provision.

There were times when she felt inferior, especially when she compared herself to others. But I saw a woman who considered no task too small. As my brother and I grew up, she focused her life on giving to us. She sacrificed her needs for the family. She learned how to drive a car after my brother and I left home. She dealt with a strong willed child – me. She stood by my Dad through the good times and the bad times.

When I was a child, she may have taken second place to my dad. He was my hero. Now that I am older, I see a beautiful, vibrant, virtuous woman. She is a Biblical Proverbs 31 woman. In my eyes, she wears a princess crown. She is my example of a mother, a wife, and a friend. Thank you for being my Mom.

FOOD FOR THOUGHT: I pray all mothers will know that they are very special people. They are not appreciated enough. We must accept that mothers are human too, and not perfect. But God knew what He was doing when He chose our mother to give birth to us. A mother's love will never stop, no matter what the child has done. As in my story above, I never appreciated my mother until I was much older. I regret that. But now I do all I can to show her that she is special to me.

JESUS, I LOVE YOU

SCRIPTURE:

Jesus said to him, "You shall love the Lord your God with all your heart, with all your soul, and with all your mind." (Matthew 22:37)

Many words have been written about you. No matter how many words we use, they don't seem sufficient to describe how wonderful you are. Even though I dig deep in my heart, words are not enough. My heart bursts forth with love for you. Sometimes I think my heart is going to break and I have to gasp for a breath.

Everything around me goes away when I look into your face. I see nothing but you. I long for the day to be with you.

My heart skips a beat when I hear your name. There is so much in that name – Jesus. You are my Savior, Lord, Deliverer, Healer, Provider, Helper, and Friend.

At the sound of your voice mountains quake, the sun stands still, waters divide, sickness leaves, and demons flee. No one compares to you. No, not one. You alone are the Alpha and the Omega.

I want to express my love, but all I can do is stand in awe. My arms are outstretched in worship of the creator of the Heavens and the Earth. I bow down to the King of Kings. I lay prostrate in humility, knowing I can't make it through the day without you. I kneel in respect to the author and the finisher of my faith. I open my mouth with laughter, because you are the joy of my life. I clap my hands to say thank you for all that you have done. I dance before you because I am unable to be still in your presence.

One touch from you is more precious than gold. I wake up in the morning and I think about you. When I go to bed at night, you are still on my mind. You are my everything.

Passion begets passion. With passion you gave your life for me. With passion I praise you, I worship you, and I love you.

FOOD FOR THOUGHT: Lord, I pray that I will never forget my first love, when I first accepted you as my Lord and Savior. My desire is to love you with a passion that grows each day. With everything that is within me, I worship you.

HIGHER GROUND

When we reach a plateau in our witness to men,
A subtle awareness is wrought from within;
A tender suggestion, His spirit comes neigh,
Our Lord's gentle prodding, how shall we reply?

Will we dwell a slave in that bitter-sweet realm,
Or answer His calling and seek higher ground;
Will we let the hurting and weeping go by;
Or ache with them and hear their heart-cry?

As our heart remains His in this love-seeking way,
He grants us a Spirit who's willing to stay;
Our spirit reborn to be humble, not proud,
His Spirit who's tested and true to the vow!

New heights are our goal as in Christ we are found,
Willing and able to find higher ground!

By Ron Massman

GOD FED THE THREE

SCRIPTURES:

Then He commanded the multitudes to sit down on the grass. And He took the five loaves and the two fish, and looking up to heaven, He blessed and broke and gave the loaves to the disciples and the disciples gave to the multitudes. Now those who had eaten were about *five thousand* men, besides women and children. (Matthew 14:19, 21)

And He took the seven loaves and the fish and gave thanks, broke them and gave them to His disciples; and the disciples gave to the multitude. Now those who ate were *four thousand* men, besides women and children. (Matthew 15: 36, 38)

When Glenn and I were first married, we both worked a daytime and a nighttime job. Our budget depended on these jobs. We lived from paycheck to paycheck. Our daughter, Kelly, was a year old when God told me to quit working and become a stay-at-home Mom. I was so full of faith, I didn't think twice. I gave my two weeks' notice.

At the time we were also new Christians and we heard that we were supposed to tithe. So we decided to claim Malachi 3:10, "'Bring all the tithes into the storehouse, that there may be food in My house, and try Me now in this,' says the Lord of hosts, 'If I will not open for you the windows of heaven and pour out for you such blessing that there will not be room enough to receive it.'"

Then we had to walk it out. I added up all the bills and compared them to the income brought in. Even after all the adjustments we made, I saw the impossible. I don't know how God did it. The freezer was always full of food. My husband would open the freezer and see meat that we didn't buy.

At the end of the month, the bills were paid. The figures showed that more money went out than came in. I can't explain it, except for the provision of God.

Throughout the years, I have seen needs met when we didn't have it. I remember one time when I had saved money to go home to see my Mom and Dad. Unexpectedly the money was needed for a family emergency. I thought I was going to have to cancel my trip. However, to my surprise I received a check for $1,000. God is our provider.

FOOD FOR THOUGHT: God is the same yesterday, today, and forever. What He did in Jesus time, He did for me and my family. When you know that God provides, you can relax and trust God.

JEHOVAH-JIREH, OUR PROVIDER

SCRIPTURE:

Then Abraham lifted his eyes and looked, and there behind him was a ram caught in a thicket by its horns. So Abraham went and took the ram, and offered it up for a burnt offering instead of his son [Isaac]. And Abraham called the name of the place, The-Lord-Will-Provide; as it is said to this day, "In the Mount of the Lord it shall be provided." (Genesis 22:13, 14)

In 1983 our family was 2,000 miles away from home, living in a tent. Our family consisted of Glenn and me, along with our two children, Kelly (7) and Alex (3). We stepped out in faith so the family could be together.

My husband, Glenn, had a chance to attend school at Fort Sam for seven weeks. The army was only paying for his way to get there. Glenn wanted to take the family with him, but we didn't know how we were going to afford it. I had created a prayer board for the trip. On this board I gathered all the possible ways to manage this great trip. I quickly became discouraged. The airplane tickets were going to cost approximately $1,300, per adult. There was no way we could afford that. A bus or train would take too long. Even traveling by car would cost money. We did not have the finances to live in a hotel for seven weeks. Each time I decided to take the prayer board off the kitchen wall, there was a nudging inside me that I was not supposed to. Then the idea came to us. The army was paying for Glenn's traveling expenses to get to San Antonio. If the family piled up in the car and traveled with Glenn, the expenses for the gas would be covered. Also, we could buy a tent, which we could afford, and the family could live in a tent while Glenn went to school. We were excited. We were going on a long journey far away from home.

We made the trip in two days, traveling day and night. We bought a tent and set up camp. While Glenn was at school during the day, the children and I played at the playground, fed the little ducks in the pond, watched the squirrels play, splashed in the swimming pool, and walked the paths of the campground. When it rained we were able to watch TV in the indoor game room. When the children took their naps, I would have my quiet time with God. On the weekends, the campground provided a Walt Disney movie for the campers. On Sundays, we attended a local church. Even though life was extremely simple, we were enjoying an adventure.

The food supply was rather limited. We did not have a refrigerator. We had a large cooler, which kept essential items, such as a loaf of bread, peanut butter, jar of jelly, butter, eggs, powdered milk and orange drink, and some crackers. We did purchase a few can goods, such as peaches and pears. Therefore, the meals were simple – usually toast and jelly for breakfast, peanut butter and jelly sandwiches and canned fruit for lunch, along with plenty of diluted Tang for the hot summer days. At night we enjoyed the main meal, when Glenn would be home to eat with us. We would go to the store and buy some hot dogs or hamburgers to cook on the camper stove.

After two weeks, the food supply was all gone. There was two more days before pay day. While Glenn went to school on Thursday, I prayed for a miracle. Otherwise, there would be no food to fill my children's hungry tummies.

Glenn came home that night with enough money to buy supper. One of the fellow students unexpectedly placed a ten dollar bill in his hand. Glenn had told no one that he needed the money. We celebrated that night over what God had provided for us.

During the seven weeks living in a tent, we experienced several miracles of God's provision.

FOOD FOR THOUGHT: Let us believe and trust God to provide our needs, even though we may not know where the answer is going to come from.

WALKING ON WATER

SCRIPTURE:

And when the disciples saw Him walking on the sea, they were troubled, saying, "It is a ghost!" And they cried out for fear.

But immediately Jesus spoke to them, saying, "Be of good cheer! It is I; do not be afraid."

And Peter answered Him and Said, "Lord, if it is You, command me to come to You on the water."

So He said, "Come." And when Peter had come down out of the boat, he walked on the water to go to Jesus.

But when he saw that the wind was boisterous, he was afraid; and beginning to sink he cried out, saying, "Lord, save me!"

And immediately Jesus stretched out His hand and caught him, and said to him, "O you of little faith, why did you doubt?" And when they got into the boat, the wind ceased. (Matthew 14:26-32)

We walk on water whenever we step out in faith to go down a path that we have never been before. We have no idea what is at the end of the path; therefore, we may be intimidated or filled with fear of the unknown. Our thoughts scream out with reasons, or excuses, for not wanting to go forward: it feels safe where we are, I am not qualified, and what if I fail, or did I hear God correctly. Below is a simple story I believe is an example in my life where I have stepped out in faith to walk on water. I didn't know what was ahead of me, and I sometimes felt the ground would give away any minute. Actually, Jesus is the Rock that we put our trust in. If He says, "Come," then we know He is there to pull us up if we begin to fall.

After our adventure living in a tent for seven weeks, my husband and I felt that God was telling us to move to Texas. We were currently living in Vermont and we had two very young children. We did not have a job waiting for either one of us. We just knew in our hearts that this is what God wanted us to do. I do admit that at one time I became fearful and questioned God's wisdom in all of this. For about a month we told God we thought the timing was wrong. We didn't have the money. Maybe we would move later when we were better financially able to make the big move. But again God showed us that this was His will in our lives. So we sold everything we owned, except for our clothes, the children's toys, my husband's table saw, and my sewing machine. We bought a simple lawn mower type utility trailer to bring our belongings. Some special items, like the painting my husband did of Jesus on the cross at Calvary, our Napoleonic chess set, our photography equipment, my special dishes and some of my books were left with our friends. Then on that faithful day we began our trip, feeling like pioneers did in times past. At the time I stated, "We are stepping out with unadulterated faith to move to an unknown place with no house or job waiting for us."

The trip took four and a half days. There were a few times that the car or trailer broke down. But we saw God marvelously provide a solution each time. One time when we were near the Texas-Arkansas border, the axle on the trailer busted. Glenn remained with the trailer while I drove to a nearby town to search for help. At the first garage I stopped at, they told me about a man who could help us. This man was able to fix our trailer. Then he invited our family to his home for a hot meal. This was a blessing.

I felt we were walking on water and Jesus pulled us up when we thought we were going to drown.

When we arrived at our destination, we lived at a camp ground for three days until we found a rent house. Glenn immediately found a job at a convenient store, which held us over until he found a carpenter's job at a church furniture factory. This was the beginning of our new life.

FOOD FOR THOUGHT: Father, I know that "walking on water" can be frightening, but we place our trust in you as we say "Yes" to the paths you want us to follow. We thank you that you will never leave us and that you are as close as a heartbeat to catch us if we begin to fall.

TESTIFY OF THE GOODNESS OF GOD

SCRIPTURES:

And they overcame him by the blood of the Lamb and by the word of their testimony. (Revelation 12:11)

Every good gift and every perfect gift is from above. (James 1:17)

When we moved from Vermont to Texas, the first thing we did, even before we found a place to live, was to find a church. We visited the church on Sunday, and on Monday we located a house to rent that was close to the church. A few days later the assistant pastor from the church visited us. As he gave the usual welcome speech, his eyes encompassed an empty house. Before he left, he prayed that my husband would find a job and that God would bless us.

The next day was the beginning of constant knocks on the door. People from the church came with food and furniture. We were overwhelmed with how the blessing of God kept flowing in. We were able to say, "Taste and see that the Lord is good" (Psalm 34:8). But this was not the end of the story.

On Christmas Eve as we responded to another knock on the door, our children were greeted by

Santa Claus holding two large, dark-green, garbage bags filled with toys and clothes. Our first Christmas away from our family was blessed by a man from the church who dressed up like Santa Claus and brought gifts to our children.

I share this story for two reasons: 1) the people of this church were an example of people who enjoyed giving, and 2) this testimony reminds me that God provides our needs.

FOOD FOR THOUGHT: Let us testify to the goodness of God. He is faithful to answer our prayers and provide our needs. Our testimonies are building blocks of faith during times of needs. When we remember how good He is, it is saying "thank you."

COMING HOME

A shadowed glimpse is all we see
Of our immortal destiny;
Shiny webs of sheer delight,
The Makers hand that holds us tight.

As ships we sail the stormy sea,
Forever longing, always free
To choose between the world and you,
Our Lord and Saviour forever true!

The cross' shadow is faithfully laid
Against our foe as war is waged;
Dark made black against the Light,
Our hope, His power, continually bright.

As we of faith more clearly see
This beacon of hope for you and for me;
We glimpse of joy, of Love divine.
These precious few moments before
our time!

By Ron Massman

ANGELS

SCRIPTURE:

The angel of the Lord encamps all around those who fear Him, and delivers them. (Psalm 34:7)

According to 2 Corinthians 4:18, the things which we cannot see (the spiritual realm) are actually more real (eternal) than the things we see with our physical eyes, which are temporal. There will be a day when the things in the spiritual realm will be seen clearly – God, Jesus, Heaven, predeceased loved ones, and angels.

The Bible includes numerous stories regarding angels. There are angels who bring messages from God to the people on Earth. In Genesis 18, three angels visited Abraham, bringing the message to him of God's plan to destroy Sodom and Gomorrah because of their depravity. In Luke 1:26-3, we are told that the angel Gabriel was sent by God to inform Mary that she was chosen to be the mother of the son of God.

Then there are angels sent by God to accomplish certain tasks. The story of "Daniel and the Lion's Den" reveals God's protection. Daniel was locked up in a lion's den because he prayed to God. Angels closed the mouths of the lions so they could not harm Daniel (see Daniel 6:22).

Angels were sent to minister to Jesus after He spent 40 days in the desert being tempted by Satan (see Matthew 4:11) and an angel appeared to Jesus in the Garden of Gethsemane to strengthen Him (see Luke 22:43).

God has even assigned angels to watch over us and to minister help to us in our hour of need and distress. According to Psalm 91:11, "He shall give his angels charge over you to keep you in all your ways." Hebrews 1:14 also states, "Are they not all ministering spirits sent forth to minister for those who will inherit salvation?"

We have heard of stories about people who have been rescued from incredible accidents. Once there was a young man, who was stuck in a car under water. Someone pulled the man out of the car to safety. Later they were unable to locate the person. The man believes it was an angel who rescued him.

A few years ago there was a story about a rapist/killer attacking women in a park of a well known city. One night a woman was walking through this park all by herself. She actually passed the killer. However, he immediately disappeared in the opposite direction. Later he revealed that he had seen two giant men walking with this lady. She had never seen the angles, but the killer did.

I have heard that babies may be able to see angels, especially before their eyes and minds become focused on this world. But as we grow and adjust to this physical world, we lose the ability to see the angles in the spiritual realm. In Matthew 18:10 Jesus said, "Take heed that you do not despise one of these little ones, for I say to you that in heaven *their angels* always see the face of My Father who is in heaven." Children have "guardian" angels watching over them and *their angels* have direct contact with God.

When we get in our car, we ask the angels to place a hedge of protection around our vehicle and protect us from any harm as we travel on the highways.

I think we will be surprised however at what an angel really looks like. We envision beautiful angels clothed in white robes and feathered wings. Just as each human being on earth is unique in appearance and purpose, angles are different in appearance and purpose: messengers, warriors, helpers, and worshipers. Even Satan was an angel at one time. We must be careful not to exalt or worship angels. The Book of Revelation depicts the angels around the throne of God worshiping Him day and night, singing, "Holy, Holy, Holy is the Lamb. Jesus is the Lamb." God has sent his angels to watch over us and to minister to us. Angels do exist.

FOOD FOR THOUGHT: I pray that we grasp the reality of the spiritual realm in its many facets. I pray that as we realize that our lives here on Earth are for a moment in time, we will be more focused on the reality of God, Jesus and the Holy Spirit. I pray that this leads us to understand the urgency to accomplish what God has called us to do. Then the day will come when the veil will be removed from our eyes and we will see the reality of our real home that now exists in the spiritual realm.

BROKEN VESSEL

SCRIPTURE:

He restores my soul; He leads me in the paths of righteousness for His name's sake. (Psalm 23:3)

Anna went through the motions of appearing all together on the outside; however, on the inside she felt like a shattered vessel, pieces scattered everywhere, unable to be put back together. "No one can help me. No one."

She had gone to church when she was a child. She had heard the children's Bible stories and memorized the Ten Commandments. But when she left home at the age of sixteen, she ran from the truth. She got caught up in the bright lights of the world and allowed herself to be seduced into the various pleasures the world could offer.

At first this lifestyle seemed exciting. Then the consequences of living recklessly came when the doctors told her she was going to be a mother. Anna declared, "No way am I going to allow a child to be born into this world."

She looked at her surroundings. Where was she? Did it matter? Her eyes studied the room that included one unkempt bed, the standard hotel bureau with mirror, and a round table with two dilapidated kitchen type chairs. This is where she called home. She was all alone.

When the drugs and alcohol didn't help her forget her decision, she contemplated suicide.

Darkness surrounded her and she did not know how to turn the light on.

She cried out to God, "If you are real, please help me." Then she thought, "He can never forgive me for what I have done."

With a glass of Jack Daniel whiskey in one hand, she poured the pills from several bottles onto the bed. She then fell to her knees beside the bed and proceeded to complete her plan to end the pain. She grabbed the first handful, but her shaking hands caused some of the pills to fall to the floor. As she leaned over to pick up the pills, her eyes fell upon a Gideon Bible that was lying in the open drawer of the stand. The sight of the book startled her. Why she did what she did next, she will never know. She opened the Bible and turned to the only scripture she could remember at that moment: John 3:16 – "For God so loved the world that He gave His only begotten Son, that whoever believes in Him should not perish but have everlasting life."

"God, you can't love me. I have done things that cannot be forgiven."

A loving God heard the cries of this young woman who was convinced that God could not forgive her. He tenderly whispered to the ears of her heart, "I do love you. I still love you. I will always love you. My son, Jesus, paid the price so that you could be free from ALL guilt. Your sin has been forgiven, never to be remembered again."

In that moment of time, Anna had a choice to make, to believe God or to believe the world and what they said about her. Anna decided. She said, "Yes. I accept Jesus as my Lord and Savior." Immediately she felt the weight of guilt leave and the arms of a loving God wrapped around her broken heart. Tears, both of repentance and joy, flowed down her face like a river washing away all the dirt and filth of an unrighteous life.

God picked up the shattered pieces of the broken vessel and restored them to a beautiful vase, where the light of God could shine through.

FOOD FOR THOUGHT: No matter what our past includes, we thank you, God, for restoring the damaged heart to a heart that beats with life, and changing us into a beautiful vessel that can be used by you.

BURYING OUR TALENTS

SCRIPTURES:

For He instructs him in right judgment, His God teaches him. (Isaiah 28:26)

He was filled with wisdom and understanding and skill in working with all kinds of bronze work. (1 Kings 7:14)

Then the Lord spoke to Moses, saying: "See, I have called by name Bezalel….and I have filled him with the Spirit of God, in wisdom, in understanding, in knowledge, and in all manner of workmanship…" (Exodus 31:1-3)

In the "Parable of the Talents" recounted by Jesus in Matthew 25:14-30, we are told of a nobleman who gave five talents to one of his servants, two talents to another, and one talent to another. The men with the five talents and two talents used their talents to double what they had. However, the man with the one talent was afraid and he buried his one talent in the ground. When the nobleman returned home from his journey, he asked the men what they had done with their talents. He was pleased with the men who had five talents and two talents because they increased what was given to them. In verses 21 and 23, he said, "Well done, good and faithful servant; you were faithful over a few things, I will make you ruler over many things. Enter into the joy of the lord." In regards to the man who hid his talent, the nobleman was angry with him.

The ability to work, whatever the job is, comes from God. Each person has a certain gift, or talent, that God has given him. We can either use that talent for the glory of God, or we can hide it. Talents may vary from singing, painting a picture, writing a story, riding a horse, or being a carpenter, to having the gift of gab, playing a sport, or bringing a smile to a person who is depressed. As we step out in whatever talent God has given us, He will bless our efforts and joy comes when we obey and please God.

When we reach the end of our lives, do we want to tell God we were afraid, so we decided to let fear keep us from doing whatever He has given us the ability to do? I sure don't. I want to hear those words: "Well done, good and faithful servant."

FOOD FOR THOUGHT: I pray we will use our God given talents to glorify Him. If anyone is afraid, I ask that our heavenly Father, with the anointing of the Holy Spirit, fill each person with the tenacity to step out and accomplish what God has given him to do.

WEEDS IN A GARDEN

SCRIPTURE:

I am the true vine, and My Father is the vine-dresser. Every branch in Me that does not bear fruit He takes away; and every branch that bears fruit He prunes, that it may bear more fruit. (John 15:1, 2)

A flower growing in God's garden is planted in good soil. The petals reach upward towards the rays of sunlight. The blossoms flourish in full glory under the master gardener's touch. Unwanted weeds may try to grow and crowd the life out of the plant, but the gardener pulls the weeds from its roots.

As God's children, we are planted in the garden of life. We submit to the gardener's precise pruning hands. He knows the right amount of fertilizer that is needed to bring life. He showers us with the rain of the Holy Spirit. He carefully prunes away the dead, unwanted weeds by its roots.

If we choose not to allow the gardener to perform his handiwork, the weeds of life can overcome us and block out the light of God. Once the weeds have overtaken us, our mind and soul may wilt from the blockage of light.

I have known the weeds of pain, anger, grief, betrayal, resentment. Unforgiveness has wrapped its roots around my heart. I have been a product of ruined fruit due to destructive weeds. I am a witness to the weeds tightening its grip on my life, choking out the truth of the Word of God.

Oh how I long for the Master's touch of His rugged, but gentle, hands. I need Him to pull out the unwanted weeds in my life. I am thirsty for the watering of the Holy Spirit, allowing His Word to restore my life so that it is productive again.

FOOD FOR THOUGHT: God, I give you permission to do a deep work, weeding out all unwanted weeds. I trust the pruning hands of God.

CITY WALLS BROKEN DOWN

SCRIPTURES:

So Satan answered the Lord and said, "Does Job fear God for nothing? Have You not made a *hedge* around him, around his household, and around all that he has on every side?" (Job 1:9, 10)

The angel of the Lord *encamps* all *around* those who fear Him, and delivers them. (Psalm 34:7)

When I was a child I knew what it was like to feel safe and secure, having no knowledge of any of the evil that existed in the world. My earthly father provided for the welfare of the house. He provided a shield (hedge) of protection around me.

Our heavenly Father also promises that He places a "hedge of protection" around those who fear Him. As children of God, if we seek Him, obey His statues, and fellowship with Him, there is a hedge that surrounds us just like walls, or a fortress, built around a city to keep the enemy (Satan) out. However, we can weaken or put holes in the walls if we do not do our part. It is our responsibility to guard them by being careful what we allow to enter in through the eye gates and ear gates of our hearts. A common phraseology expresses this thought – garbage in/garbage out.

Take this simple example, if we listen to depressing music all the time, we are allowing depressive thoughts to enter into our minds and subsequently we could become depressed. We weaken these walls of protection by allowing the negative thoughts in. God is unable to protect us from depression as long as we keep allowing the depressing music inside our walls. If we continue to allow this destructive force in, then the walls, or hedge of protection, are broken down. When they are broken down, Satan can play havoc with our lives.

There are many other areas where we allow holes in our walls of protection. We need to be careful of what we watch on television, listen to on the radio, or read. Places where we hang out or people we associate with can affect these invisible walls that surround us.

It is very important to protect the walls of our hearts so that we don't open a doorway for Satan to enter in.

FOOD FOR THOUGHT: Father, we want to keep our hearts pure so that Satan does not have a way to enter in and play havoc with our lives. We ask the Holy Spirit to show us areas where the walls have become weak by "garbage" that has entered in through the eye gates and ear gates of our hearts.

ARE WE THERE YET – PATIENCE

SCRIPTURE:

My brethren, count it all joy when you fall into various trials, knowing that the testing of your faith produces patience. But let patience have its perfect work, that you may be perfect and complete, lacking nothing. (James 1: 2-4)

We are all probably acquainted with the scenario of a family in a car who is going on a long trip and a child asks, "Are we there yet?" Five minutes later the child asks again, "Are we there yet?" The child becomes more impatient the longer it takes to get to their destination. He keeps asking the same question over and over. The redundant question does not help the family get "there" any faster. The distance is a constant factor.

I have been guilty of displaying the same amount of impatience when waiting for a response to a problem. I want the answer now, not tomorrow, not a month from now, nor a year from now. I want the breakthrough now.

In the past I have been known to lose my temper. Sometimes I have let frustration affect my attitude, which in turn caused me to allow my addictive habits to be controlled by my emotions. For example, when I get frustrated, I tend to eat. Many years ago, I used to smoke cigarettes. My husband was a smoker also.

He knew that smoking was bad, but he enjoyed smoking, especially the action of exhaling. It made him feel like he was exhaling stress. I definitely understood what he meant. Neither response to stress is the solution.

I am not keen on suffering or walking through the valleys of problems that God says will help me to grow in Him. However, there are many situations where it is impossible for the response to come now. So what do I do while I wait?

Book of Hebrews, chapters 3 and 4, talks about the *promise of rest*. God rested on the seventh day from all His works. There remains therefore a rest for the people of God. "For he who has entered His rest has himself also ceased from his works as God did from His" (Hebrews 4:10).

God says we are to rest in Him. We are to release the problem to Him. We are not to pick it back up. The answer could come in a day. It could take a week, a month, a year, or several years before we see the answer manifest. During that time, we are to trust in God, wait without fretting, relax, and enjoy life. God's answer is always better than ours.

FOOD FOR THOUGHT: Others, like me, tend to be fretful when we don't hold the reins of our lives in our own hands. Actually God's Word in Hebrews explains that it is a sin if we don't rest in God. Father God, I pray that we learn to let go of the reins, trust you, and rest in you – this is the desire of your heart.

MY LEGACY

SCRIPTURE:

Do not lay up for yourselves treasures on Earth, where moth and rust destroy and where thieves break in and steal; but lay up for yourselves treasures in Heaven, where neither moth nor rust destroys and where thieves do not break in and steal. For where your treasure is, there your heart will be also. (Matthew 6:19-21)

My greatest wish is that when my children and friends think about the person who I am, I want them to see...

Someone who loves God with her whole heart,
Someone who stands strong in battle,
Someone who is a servant of God,
Someone who prays,
Someone who has strong faith,
Someone who is a worshipper of God,
Someone who is a giver,
Someone who is a helper,
Someone who is known for her word,
Someone who obeys the statutes of God,
Someone who talks to God,
Someone who is diligent, disciplined, and devoted,
Someone who is loyal to her family and friends,
Someone who touches the lives of others,

Someone who helps people to come out of darkness and into the light, and
Someone who is a soul winner.

This is the legacy I want to leave behind for my family and friends, a woman who loved and served God visibly so that my actions encouraged and brought other people closer to God.

FOOD FOR THOUGHT: Father God, I pray that my life is an example to others. I pray that my words and my actions lead people to you, not away from you. I pray that at the end of my time here on Earth, I will hear my God say, "Well done."

ENJOY EACH OTHER

SCRIPTURE:

Therefore be imitators of God as dear children, and walk in love, as Christ also has loved us and given Himself for us. (Ephesians 5:1, 2)

My little girl pulls on my pant leg, requesting my attention. For what seems the zillionth time, she wants me to read *Green Eggs and Ham.* Impatiently, I respond, "Later, honey, Mommy is busy right now." But when later comes, I am detained with what I believe are important duties. So my little girl is entertained by the television.

My sweet husband decided, for no reason at all, to buy me a dozen red roses. My thankful response was, "They are beautiful, but we really can't afford to waste money on perishable flowers." The sad look in his eyes reflected his disappointment, but the damaging words had already been released from my mouth.

The phone rang. I noticed on the ID Caller that it was the widow from church. I understood she is still grieving and needs someone to talk to, but I really don't have the time right now to listen. So I don't answer the phone.

My spouse enjoys eating out once in a while, but I feel it is a waste of money. After my many badgering discussions on the matter, I believe he has finally received the message that it is more frugal to eat home cooked meals.

My husband enjoys fishing and hunting and football games. I enjoy reading romance novels and watching the Hallmark channel. My husband does his thing, while I do mine. I know we should spend time together, but we don't enjoy each other's hobbies.

My Mom and Dad live so far away. They seem like strangers. Maybe I should call them more often. Maybe I should write them a letter. Maybe next week when I have more time.

My little girl is grown up and has her own family. My husband became very ill and went to be with the Lord a few years ago. Where did the time go?

My granddaughter pulls on my pant leg, requesting my attention. She wants me to read *Green Eggs and Ham*. I respond, "Nana would love to read to you. I have plenty of time for you."

FOOD FOR THOUGHT: I pray that we will not let the business of life stop us from taking time to love and enjoy each other.

FATHER GOD, THANK YOU

SCRIPTURE:

In everything give thanks; for this is the will of God in Christ Jesus for you. (1 Thessalonians 5:18)

Above all, Father God thank you for coming after this lost sheep. No words are sufficient in thanking you for loving me when I turned my back on you. I rebelled against all I was taught because I was so angry at you for all the hypocrisy and hurt in the world. I ran from you, because the pain inside me caused me to blame you for it all. But you never left my side. Through time and patience, the veil was removed from my eyes and your love penetrated the walls that were built up around me. When I returned to you, you didn't remind me of my past; you gave me hope for a future. Your salvation from death and darkness is priceless. Father God, I thank you for your son, Jesus, who made the way for me to return to you.

There was a time when I fell into a pit of depression. I couldn't see your light. Only darkness surrounded me. The devil thought for sure that he had me this time and that he had stolen me from you. He bombarded my mind with words of destruction, which found its way to my heart. These lies of the devil were truth to my mind. I saw no hope. But God! You were always there in the shadows, even though

I could not sense your presence. You surprised the devil, when you destroyed his tactics with your intervention of love, healing and hope. The devil lost and you won the battle for me. Father, I thank you that you were there and saved me from drowning in the sea of depression that would have led me to death.

Father, I also want to thank you for the mate you brought into my life. You gave me thirty years where we walked the path of life together. You blessed us with two beautiful children, a gift of indescribable love. For every door we opened, you were always there with the provision. When challenges came, you stuck by us and showed us the solution. The many adventures you brought us through have left an album of pictures in my memory. Thank you, Father, for the love that tied our hearts together with a cord that could not be broken.

The road of my dearly beloved husband came to an end with a sickness that led to death. I had to let go of him, whom I loved with my whole heart and who gave me purpose. Grief came. But your mercy and grace surrounded me until I could stand again. Thank you, Father, for holding my hand when I was unable to hold myself up.

When my health became a danger to my own life, you showed me what I needed to do to restore my health. I thank you for the Word of God that I stand on each day for my healing.

Father, I am grateful you were with me when I went down that path of my second marriage that regretfully led to divorce. I thank you that as in Jeremiah 29:11 you reminded me you have good plans for my life. Thank you for revealing to me that I can still have purpose and a reason to wake up in the morning.

I have made mistakes on this road to my final destination with you. But you have always made my crooked paths straight and washed me with your forgiveness. When I could see no way out, you came forth with the answer better than I could have dreamed of. Father, thank you for taking care of me.

Of course, I thank you for the air I breathe. I take nothing for granted. I know all the blessings come from you. Father, I thank you for your love that endures forever.

FOOD FOR THOUGHT: I pray that each and every day that we remember to thank God for that day and everything in it. All blessings come from God.

AS I LAY ME DOWN TO SLEEP

SCRIPTURES:

But God came to Abimelech in a dream by night; and said to him... (Genesis 20:3)

At Gibeon, the Lord appeared to Solomon in a dream by night; and God said... (I Kings 3:5)

An angel of the Lord appeared to Joseph in a dream, saying... (Matthew 2:13)

Lord, as I lay me down to sleep, I thank you for helping me through another day. As each day passes, I know it is closer to the day when I will see my Lord face to face. But until then, I don't want to face a day without you by my side. Even as I sleep, I pray my dreams are filled with your presence, giving me thoughts and ideas that will help me fulfill my destiny here on Earth. I ask that fear and despair does not enter the portals of my dream world, only your creative power at work in my dreams.

As I sleep, I know rest and healing comes to my body, per your omniscient and omnipotent plan for us in creation. My body is intricately designed. Even though I am asleep, each part of my body still functions according to your divine purpose. Nothing is done by my hand. My heart beats and my lungs breathe, all because of you. Again, I thank you for taking care of me while I sleep.

Tomorrow will be a new day. I will wake up refreshed and ready to start another day with excitement and anticipation, knowing it will be a great day. Any mistakes from yesterday are of the past. I take one day at a time. My future is not yet today.

Lord, as I lay me down to sleep, I say, "Good night." The last thought I want before I enter the dream world is you.

FOOD FOR THOUGHT: As the song we sang when we were little, "As I lay me down to sleep, I pray the Lord my soul to keep." I pray that my sleep will be peaceful and that my dreams are directed by you.

CROWNS IN OUR GLORY

When we get to Heaven, what glory we'll see!
Our Lord face to face in His great majesty.
The brightness in Him will be found in that day
A light encompassing, true Love on display.

Will we, as we praise Him and sing the new song,
Have multiplied blessings in that day so long?
Or will we reap stubble that burns and decays.
No longer a form our refiner can save?

Will crowns thrown before Him be tarnished and old,
Or some clean and spotless, new victories told?
As servants who loved Him on earth will we be,
Or fools who elected to bark our own tree?

Will we, as He holds us and whispers our name,
Recall the sweet triumphs for Jesus, not fame?
Remember those trials that once proved us to be
Yielded and faithful for all men to see?

We must as we seek His great will in our lives,
Keep Christ in the forefront, these crowns to our side.
No goal could be better, no service too small,
These crowns in our glory, Christ honors them all!

By Ron Massman

APPENDIX

NAMES OF GOD

REFERENCES:

1. King James Version
2. http://biblos.com
3. *The Strong's Exhaustive Concordance of the Bible*, 1890
4. http://strongsnumbers.com
5. http://en.wikipedia.org/wiki/Names_of_God_in_Judaism
6. http://larryleaministries.net/LordsPrayerOutline.pdf

NAMES OF GOD:

1. **Jehovah** (Yhvh) http://strongsnumbers.com/hebrew/3068.htm (proper name of the God of Israel)

Genesis 6:3 And I appeared unto Abraham, unto Isaac, and unto Jacob, by the name of God Almighty, but by the name *Je-ho-vah* was I not know to them. http://biblos.com/exodus/6-3/htm

Yah-weh   3068   Lord

Strong's Concordance 3068 (Y'hovah, yeh-ho-vaw) from 1961; (the) self-Existent or Eternal; Jehovah, Jewish national name of God – Jehovah, the Lord.

2. **Yahweh** (YHWH) http://strongsnumbers.com/hebrew/1961.htm (Be)

Exodus 3:14 And God said unto Moses, *I AM THAT I AM*; and he said, Thus shalt thou say unto the children of Israel, *I AM* hath sent me unto you. http://biblos.com/exodus/3-14/htm

Eh-yeh   1961   I AM

Strong's Concordance 1961 (hayah, haw-yaw) a primitive root; to exist, i.e. be or become, come to pass.

3. **EL OHIM** http://strongsnumbers.com/hebrew/430.htm (God)

Genesis 1:1 In the beginning *God* created the heaven and the earth. http://biblos.com/genesis/1-1/htm

E-lo-him	430	God

Strong's Concordance <u>430</u> (elohiym, *el-o-heem*) plural of 433; gods in the ordinary sense; but specifically used (in the plural thus, especially with the article) of the supreme God.

4. **ROI** <u>http://strongsnumbers.com/hebrew/7473.</u> <u>htm</u> (shepherd)

Psalm 23:1 The Lord *is my shepherd*; I shall not want. <u>http://biblos.com/psalms/23-1.htm</u>

Yah-weh	3068	The Lord
Ro-'i	7462	is my shepherd

Strong's Concordance <u>7473</u> (ro'iy, *ro-ee*) from active participle of 7462; pastoral; as noun, a shepherd. <u>7462</u> (ra'ah, raw-aw) a primitive root; to tend a flock.

5. **JIREH** <u>http://strongsnumbers.com/hebrew/7200.</u> <u>htm</u> (to see)

Genesis 22:8, 14 And Abraham said, My son, *God will provide* himself a lamb for a burnt-offering: so they both went together…And Abraham called the name of that place *Jehovahjireh*; as it is said to this day, In the mount of the Lord it shall be seen. <u>http://</u> <u>biblos.com/genesis/22-8.htm</u> and <u>http://biblos.com/</u> <u>genesis/22-14.htm</u>.

E-lo-him	430	God
Yir-'eh	7200	will provide
Yah-weh	3068	The Lord
Yir-'eh	7200	will Provide

Strong's Concordance 7200 (ra'ah, *raw-aw*) a primitive root; to see. 3070 (Y'hovah yireh, *yeh-ho-vaw yir-eh*) from 3068 and 7200, Jehovah will see (to it).

6. **ADONAI** http://strongsnumbers.com/hebrew/ 113.htm (Lord)

Psalm 97:5 The hills melted like wax at the presence *of the Lord*, at the Presence *of the Lord* of the whole earth. http://biblos.com/psalms/97-5.htm

| Yah-weh | 3068 | of the Lord |
| A-do-vn | 113 | of the Lord |

Strong's Concordance 3068 (Y'hovah, *yeh-ho-vaw*) from 1961; (the) self-Existent or Eternal; Jehovah, Jewish national name of God. 113 (adown, *aw-done*, or (shorter) adon, *aw-done*); from an unused root (mean to rule); sovereign, i.e. controller (human or divine); lord, master, owner.

7. **SHALOM** http://strongsnumbers.com/hebrew/ 7965.htm (completeness, soundness, welfare, peace)

Judges 6:24 Then Gideon built an altar there unto the Lord, and called it *Jehovah-shalom*. http://biblos. com/judges/6-24.htm

| Yah-weh | 3068 | of the Lord |
| Shal-lo-vm | 7965 | is Peace |

Strong's Concordance 7965 (shalowm, *shaw-lome*) or shalom from 7999; safe, i.e. (figurative) well, happy, friendly; also (abstract) welfare, i.e. health, prosperity, peace.

8. **ROPHE** http://strongsnumbers.com/hebrew/7495. htm (to heal)

Isaiah 53:5 But he was wounded for our transgressions, he was bruised for our iniquities: the chastisement of our peace was upon him and with his stripes we are *healed*. http://biblos.com/isaiah/53-5.htm

| Nir-pa- | 7495 | are healed |

Strong's Concordance 7495 (rapha, *raw-faw*) a primitive root; properly to mend (by stitching), i.e. (figuratively) to cure: cure, (cause to) heal, physician, repair, make whole.

9. **TSIDKENU** http://strongsnumbers.com/hebrew/ 3072.htm (the Lord our righteousness)

Jeremiah 23:5, 6 Behold, the days come, saith the Lord, that I will raise unto David a *righteous* Branch, and a King shall reign and prosper and shall execute judgment and justice in the earth.

In his days Judah shall be saved, and Israel shall dwell safely; and this is his name whereby he shall be called, *THE LORD OUR RIGHTEOUSNESS.* http://biblos.com/jeremiah/23-5.htm ; http://biblos. com/jeremiah/23-6.htm

Tsad-dik	6662	a righteous
Yah-weh	3068	the Lord
Tzid-ke-nu	6664	prosperity

Strong's Concordance 3072 (Y'hovah tsidqenuw, *yeh-ho-vaw tsid-kay-noo*) from 3068 and 6664 with pronoun suffix; Jehovah (is) our right; Jehovah-Tsidkenu, a symbolical epithet of the Messiah and of Jesus: the Lord our righteousness. 6662 (tsaddiyq, *tsad-deek*) from 6663; just, lawful, righteous (man).

10. **SHAMMAH** http://strongsnumbers.com/ hebrew/8033.htm (there, thither)

Ezekiel 48:35 It was round about eighteen thousand measures; and the name of the city from that day shall be, *The Lord is there.* http://biblos.com/eze-kiel/48-35.htm :

Sham-mah	8033	in it

Strong's Concordance 8033 (sham,shawm) a primitive participle (rather from the relative 834) there. 3074 (Y'hovah shammah, yeh-ho-vaw shawm-maw) from 3068 and 8033 with directive enclitic; Jehovah (is) there; Jehovah-Shammah, a symbol, title of Jesus.

11. **NISSI** http://strongsnumbers.com/hebrew/5251. htm (a standard, ensign, signal, sign)

Exodus 17:15 And Moses built an altar, and called the name of it *Jehovah-nissi.* http://biblos.com/exodus/17-15.htm

Yah-weh	3068	the Lord
Nis-si	5251	is my Banner

Strong's Concordance 5251 (nec, *nace*) from 5264; a flag, also a sail; by implication a flagstaff; generally, a signal; figuratively, a token: - banner, pole, sail, (en)-sign, standard. 3071 (Y'hovah nicciy, *yeh-ho-vaw nis-see*) from 3068 and 5251; Jehovah (is) my banner; Jehovah-Nissi, a symbolical name of an altar in the Desert.

12. **MEKADDESH (M'KADDESH)** http://strongsnumbers.com/hebrew/6942.htm (to be set apart or consecrated)

Leviticus 20:8 And ye shall keep my statutes, and do them: I am the Lord which *sanctify* you. http://biblos.com/leviticus/20-8.htm

Yah-weh	3068	the Lord
Me-kad-dish-chem	6942	sanctifies

Strong's Concordance 6942 (qadash, *kaw-dash*) appoint, bid, consecrate, dedicate, defile, hallow, (be, keep) holy, prepare, proclaim, purify, sanctify (-ied one, self), wholly.

13. **EL SHADDAI** http://strongsnumbers.com/hebrew/410.htm (God) and http://strongsnumbers.com/hebrew/7706.htm (Almighty)

Genesis 17:1 When Abram was ninety years old and nine, the Lord appeared to Abram, and said unto him, I am the *Almighty God*; walk before me, and be thou perfect. http://biblos.com/genesis/17-1.htm

El	410	God
Shad-dai	7706	Almighty

Strong's Concordance 410 (el, *ale*) short, from 352; strength; as adjective mighty; especially the Almighty God (but used also of any deity); God. 7706 (Shadday, *shad-dah ee*) from 7703, the Almighty.

14. **ABBA** http://stgrongsnumbers.com/greek/5.htm (Abba)

Galatians 4:6 And because ye are sons, God hath sent forth the Spirit of his Son into your hearts, crying, *Abba, Father.* http://biblos.com/galatians/4-6.htm

Abba	5	Abba
Pater	3962	Father

Strong's Concordance 5 (Abba, *ab-bah*); of Chaldee; father (as a vocative); ABBA. <u>3962 </u>(pater, *pat-ayr*); apparently a primary word; a "father" (literally or figuratively, near or more remote); father, parent.

ABOUT THE AUTHORS

*C**laudette Ann (Lizotte) Miller** was born in Newport, Vermont. She received her Bachelor of Science in Education at the University of Vermont in the fall of 1971. Since she graduated in mid season, she started working in the payroll department at Ethan Allen Furniture in Orleans, Vermont. She was married to Glenn Miller in 1974 and they were blessed with two beautiful children. In 1983 the family decided to move to Waco, Texas where she spent twenty-two years at American Income Life Insurance Company as a correspondent clerk and claims adjuster. Glenn battled with a serious illness for almost four years and in 2001 he went to be with the Lord. She remarried in 2003; however, the marriage ended in divorce in 2007. Now as a retired widow, she lives with her daughter and son-in-law in the Dallas area, helping raise her two grandchildren. She is a graduate of the Long Ridge Writers Group's course "Breaking into Print" and a member of the North Texas Christian Writer's Group. She has been published in the nostalgia magazine, *Oxford SO &*

SO and the online magazine *Mentoring Moments for Christian Women.*

Ron Massman was born November 25, 1945 in Waco, Texas into the "post war baby boomer" generation. He grew up in the culture of the '50's and '60's. After graduating from high school, he attended two years of college. Still unaware at that time of God's calling, at age twenty-two he pursued a career working for AT&T, which continues to this day. Three years later began eleven years of marriage ending in divorce, plunging him into unknown territory. Because of this, he started becoming aware of God's calling on his life. His "uneventful" life suddenly took on a new meaning. Having made Christ lord of his life, he has seen his three children accept Jesus as lord and savior. Teaching God's Word and writing of His Love for His children has opened up blessings in every area of service. God's guidance led him to a woman who shares his passion for the things of Christ and His church. Linda and Ron became one in the bond of matrimony in the year of 2003, and continue to serve the Lord in His Kingdom until He comes.

CPSIA information can be obtained at www.ICGtesting.com
Printed in the USA
LVOW072112080512

280799LV00001B/2/P